Margaret Fulton
slow cooking

Margaret Fulton
slow cooking

NEW HOLLAND

contents

Margaret Fulton, OAM, was born in Scotland and has since become a cooking 'guru', writer, journalist, author, and commentator. Her original *The Margaret Fulton Cookbook*, first published in 1968 sold over 1.5 million copies and taught generations how to cook and entertain. Her early recipes encouraged housewives to vary the staples, to be creative with food and 'discover' food from exotic places such as Spain, Italy, India and China. As Cookery Editor, she brought these into homes through her articles in magazines and her regular appearances on various TV shows. She remains committed to good, wholesome food and continues to appear in magazines and television campaigns.

introduction to slow cooking

The inspiration for the modern electric slow cooker were the iron and clay cooking pots, which were among the earliest utensils used by cooks of many countries. The virtue of these pots and the materials used is the way they slowly absorb heat, retain it and then slowly transfer it to their contents, so that food at the top of the pot is cooked just as thoroughly on the top as the bottom, while only a low heat is required.

I first introduced readers to the 'crock-pot' in 1976. The pot and the book were a success. This book is an update of the original *Crock-Pot Cookbook,* and the recipes transfer naturally to suit today's slow cookers.

Simple healthy stews and casseroles and classic dishes like the Beef bourguignonne and Coq au vin are all naturals in a slow cooker. Pork becomes juicy and succulent; a leg of lamb with good old-fashioned onion gravy never tasted so good. You can make puddings in a slow cooker, pots of soup, and create delicious chicken dishes ranging from a whole roast chicken to chicken pieces in a sauce, like Chicken cacciatore. Vegetables, rice and hearty side dishes are also brought to slow-cooked perfection. The slow cooker however, really does come into its own cooking wonderful stews and casseroles. In particular, the cheaper cuts of meat take on a lovely tenderness that simply melts in your mouth.

In a slow cooker, food can cook for hours unattended, leaving you plenty of time to get on with your daily activities. If you're a working parent, the evening meal becomes no problem at all. With a little preparation you can have a dish that has simmered and cooked all day on the table 10 minutes after you walk in the door.

Enjoy your slow cooker, make it work for you and discover how good food can taste when it's prepared in this modern, up-to-date version of the traditional cooking-pot.

Happy cooking and good eating.

Margaret Fulton

perfect slow-cooked dishes every time

Always read the manufacturer's instructions for the use and care of your slow cooker – this is most important for keeping it in good condition. Don't fill your slow cooker any higher than 2 cm (1 inch) from the top, even though this might mean adding less liquid than the recipe states, as proper heat distribution cannot be guaranteed when the slow cooker is too full. The temperature within a slow cooker will vary with the type of food being cooked. Since slow cooking is done at a very low temperature, it is important that all the food inside a slow cooker becomes hot enough to cook properly, thus preventing possible food spoilage.

Remember liquids do not 'boil away' as in other methods of cooking, so usually you'll have more liquid at the end of the cooking process instead of less. One cup of liquid is enough for any recipe unless it contains rice or pasta, or if you are cooking 'boiled' meats like corned beef. Removing the cover and setting a slow cooker on High for about 15 minutes before serving can reduce excess liquid. Most recipes cooked on Low will be juicier than usual, since the Low setting prevents the boiling away of flavoursome liquids.

Always cook with the cover on, except in the case of baking or cooking puddings when the lid may be tilted, or the vent in a slow cooker lid opened (if the model has one). Your slow cooker performs best if undisturbed. Lifting the lid can lengthen the cooking time; if you need to stir, do it during the last hour of cooking time.

The specific times in these recipes (like 6 to 10 hours) may seem a bit loose, but basically, timing is not critical with slow cooker cookery, particularly when cooking on the Low setting. In four hours the food would be 'done'. But in four more hours it would be done a little more and be a little more tender – depending on the dish being cooked. Cooking small portions in your slow cooker is perfectly all right, but cooking times will vary. To work properly, your slow cooker needs to be at least one-third full for cooking to conform to recommended times, unless the recipe states otherwise.

When cooking small amounts of food with little moisture, place a light covering of aluminium foil on top of the food to retain all the moisture. The use of foil is also recommended during roasting when the vegetables are not covered by meat or liquid. Just wrap the vegetables in foil and place them around the edge of the slow cooker where the element runs. If you are roasting meat or cooking fish without water, simply cook on Low.

Most meat will cook well in a slow cooker, but will not brown as they do in a conventional oven, unless you brown them beforehand. Visible fat should be trimmed from cuts of meat before being put in the slow cooker. The more fat or marbling meat has, the more liquid you will end up with. Simply scoop fat from the surface with a spoon or use a slice of white bread to absorb excess oil just before serving. Or, if you have time, let the dish cool and refrigerate overnight and then simply remove any solidified fat the next day.

A slow cooker needs little or no attention. The heat is so low, the food does not need to be continually stirred to keep it from burning, unless where directed in the recipe. So do try to curb a natural inclination to lift the lid, as doing so does increase the cooking time by about 20 minutes. Because of the low temperatures used in a slow cooker, it is an extremely economical and safe way to cook; the energy used is similar to an average light bulb, and the steam created within the tightly covered slow cooker effectively destroys bacteria.

Thaw any frozen foods before putting them into the slow cooker. If preparing dishes the evening before, place ingredients in snap lock bags or containers rather than in the slow cooker insert, as a cold insert will take extra time to heat up and can add to the cooking time.

Slow cookers vary in size and styles; most have a ceramic crock insert, while others come with a heat-resistant insert which can be used on direct heat. These models make browning meat so much easier. Slow cooker controls vary, some are digital, others manual, but most have a Low and High setting. Generally, food cooked on Low take double the time of dishes cooked on High. Some slow cookers have an automatic setting, and a 'keep warm' or 'hold' setting. The automatic setting will start cooking on High, then switch to Low after an optimum temperature has been reached. 'Keep warm' or hold will keep the temperature of the food at a ready to serve temperature, while you prepare side dishes and until you are ready to eat.

Like your refrigerator however, any interruptions to power supply will affect cooking and food safety. If power is disrupted for a length of time it is advised that food left sitting partially uncooked or at room temperature for any extended period is not consumed.

Once you understand your slow cooker, through cooking recipes that have already been worked out for you in this book, it will be possible to adapt other recipes – your own old and new favourites. When converting recipes, refer to your manufacturer's guide for details.

guide to weights and measurements

---

1 teaspoon = 5g/5ml

1 tablespoon = Australian: 20g/20ml; NZ, South Africa, USA: 15g/15ml

We have used Australian tablespoons

Liquid measures: 1 cup = 250ml (9fl oz)

Solid measures (vary, depending on substance): 1 cup caster sugar = 220g (8oz); 1 cup flour = 150g (5oz)

1 cup white sugar = 220g (8oz)

converting oven or cooktop recipes

CONVENTIONAL RECIPE TIMING

15 to 30 minutes

35 to 45 minutes

50 minutes to 3 hours

SLOW COOKER TIMING

1½ to 2½ hours on High or 3 to 6 hours on Low

3 to 4 hours on High or 6 to 8 hours on Low

4 to 6 hours on High or 8 to 12 hours on Low

stocks & soups

———⦿———

Making a basic beef, chicken or vegetable stock is easy in a slow cooker. Use stock to add flavour to gravies and casseroles, and to make excellent soups.

Delicious stock can be made from meat trimmings, ham or bacon bones, or chicken frames, and parts of vegetables you often throw out like celery leaves, vegetable peelings and parsley stalks, along with a chopped onion or two.

Some soups require a rich stock as a base while others are made with water and vegetables, with butter and herbs to give them their flavour.

Soup is a first course, or a meal in itself. Who can resist a hearty soup on a cold winter night?

When making soup or a dish with a lot of liquid remember not to fill the slow cooker higher than 2cm (1 inch) from the top.

beef stock

Makes: 3 litres (5 pints)

Cooking time: 10–12 hours on Low; 4–6 hours on High

soup bones such as shin or shoulder

250g (8oz) chopped shin beef

2 celery stalks or celery leaves

small piece each of turnip, carrot and parsnip

4 peppercorns

1 small onion

bouquet garni (see below)

3 litres (5 pints) cold water (or less depending on the size of the slow cooker)

salt to taste

Ask your butcher to split the bones. Remove any meat and chop finely. Wash the bones and place in the slow cooker with chopped meat, vegetables and seasonings. Fill the slow cooker by two-thirds with cold water (do not fill to the brim). Cover and cook overnight on Low, or 10 to 12 hours on Low, or 4 to 6 hours on High. If cooked on High the stock will be lighter in colour and less concentrated.

Remove bones and strain stock into a basin. When cool, skim the fat from the surface and store stock in the refrigerator.

The stock keeps well for about a week, or it may be frozen for longer periods.

Bouquet Garni: You can buy this mixture or make one yourself. It is a group of herbs consisting of a bay leaf, sprig of thyme, tarragon, chervil (or any other fresh herb available), 3 or 4 parsley stalks, half a carrot and a small celery stalk all tied together in a piece of muslin. A bouquet is easier to remove from the finished dish than stray leaves.

Note: If you are wanting a brown, rich beef stock, brown the bones and meat beforehand in 2 tablespoons of vegetable oil. This can be done in the oven or on the stove top.

chicken stock

Makes: 3 litres (5 pints)
Cooking time: 8–10 hours on Low; 2–3 hours on High

1.2kg (2¼lb) boiling fowl, chicken pieces (such as wings, necks or backs) or chicken frames

2 celery stalks, including leaves

small piece each of turnip, carrot and parsnip

4 peppercorns

1 small onion

bouquet garni (see Beef stock recipe)

3 litres (5 pints) cold water (or less depending on the size of the slow cooker)

salt to taste

Wash the bones and place in the slow cooker with vegetables and seasonings. Fill the slow cooker by two-thirds with cold water (do not fill to the brim). Cover and cook overnight 8–10 hours on Low, or 2–3 hours on High. If cooked on High setting, the stock will be lighter in colour and less concentrated.

Remove bones and strain stock into a basin. When cool, skim fat from the surface and store stock in the refrigerator.

The stock keeps well for up to a week, or it may be frozen for much longer periods.

vegetable stock

1 leek

2 celery stalks or celery leaves

1 onion, halved

1 small piece each of turnip, carrot and parsnip,
    chopped

4 peppercorns

1 small onion, halved

3 litres (5 pints) cold water (or less, depending
    on the size of the slow cooker)

salt to taste

Fill the slow cooker by two-thirds with cold water (do not fill to the brim). Remove dark green part of leek and slice the remainder thinly. Add all the vegetables and seasonings. Cover and cook for 4 to 6 hours on Low, 2 hours on High.

The stock keeps well for up to a week in an airtight container in the fridge, or it may be frozen for much longer periods.

NOTE: Mushrooms and whole garlic cloves are good additions for a vegetable stock. If you like a stock with Asian flavours, add green onions, ginger slices and fresh coriander roots.

soup garnishes

A garnish or accompaniment is served with soup to add flavour, provide a contrast in texture and give eye appeal or to make the soup a more substantial dish.

Make your own croutons by frying small cubes of sliced bread in butter or oil. Or, toast bread and cut it into small squares. Another option is to cut bread into crescent shapes with a round cutter, brush with oil and bake in a hot oven (200°C/400°F) for 10 minutes.

Melba toasts are thin slices of bread lightly baked in the oven. Remove the crusts, then slice in half, diagonally. Split each half through the centre horizontally with a sharp knife. Place on baking tray and cook in moderate oven (180°C/375°F) for 15 minutes until golden and crisp.

Other garnishes are parsley, snipped chives, or other herbs including basil, coriander (cilantro), crumbled crispy fried bacon, grated cheese, a swirl of cream or dollop of sour cream or plain yoghurt, paper-thin slices of radish or carrot, or a sprinkle of ground paprika.

vegetable soup

Serves: 6-8

Cooking time: 7–8 hours on Low

45g (1½oz) butter

2 large onions, finely chopped

2 large carrots, finely diced

4 large potatoes

1 celery stalk, sliced

6 cups of stock

salt and freshly ground black pepper to taste

1 cup milk

1 tablespoon plain flour

1 tablespoon butter

1 tablespoon chopped parsley to serve

Melt butter in a medium saucepan, add vegetables, cover and cook gently for 10 to 15 minutes, shaking pan occasionally.

Place in the slow cooker with stock and seasonings. Cover and cook on Low for 6 to 8 hours.

If liked, thicken with milk, flour and butter mixed together. Add to slow cooker and turn onto High setting for 15 to 20 minutes or until thickened.

When ready to serve, sprinkle with parsley.

scotch broth

3 lamb shanks, halved

6 cups of stock

½ cup pearl barley, washed

1 onion, finely chopped

2 carrots, diced

2 celery stalks, sliced

1 small piece of swede, parsnip or turnip, diced

salt and freshly ground black pepper, to taste

finely chopped parsley to serve

Place shanks in slow cooker with stock and barley.

Prepare vegetables and add to slow cooker, cover and set on Low and cook for 8 to10 hours.

Lift shanks from cooker and remove the meat. Discard the bones and dice the meat, removing any surplus fat or gristle. Skim any fat from the top of the soup, add diced meat to slow cooker.

Check for seasoning and serve very hot, sprinkled with parsley.

leek and potato soup

Serves: 6-8

Cooking time: 6–8 hours on Low; 3–4 hours on High

4 potatoes

2 leeks

2 onions, chopped

1 celery stalk, sliced

3 cups chicken stock

2 cups water

60g (2oz) butter

3 teaspoons salt

1 cup cream (or low fat cream)

chopped chives, to serve

Peel potatoes and cut into small dice. Remove dark green part of leek and slice the remainder thinly.

Reserve 1 cup of sliced leek. Place vegetables in the slow cooker with stock, two cups of water, butter, salt and pepper. Cover and cook on Low for 6 to 8 hours, or High 3 to 4 hours.

Twenty minutes before serving, stir in cream and reserved leeks. If a smooth soup is required, mash with a potato masher or puree in a blender before adding cream. Serve garnished with chives.

VARIATION: *Vichyssoise*
Make as for Leek and potato soup up to end of cooking time. Allow soup to cool then puree in a blender or push through a fine sieve. Stir in cream and chill. To serve, top with a spoonful of cream and a sprinkle of chives or parsley. Vichyssoise may also be served hot.

pumpkin soup

90g (3oz) butter

1kg (2lb) pumpkin, peeled and chopped

1 small onion, chopped

3 cups water or chicken stock

2 cups milk

1 tablespoon plain flour

grated nutmeg to taste

sour cream or croutons and chopped parsley
to serve

Melt two-thirds of the butter in a heavy pan, add pumpkin and onion, cover and cook gently for 10 minutes. Place in slow cooker, add water or stock, cover and cook on Low for 6 to 8 hours.

Puree in a blender or push through a sieve. Return to slow cooker, add milk and remaining butter blended with flour, and nutmeg. Stir well, cover and cook on High for 15 to 20 minutes or until thick and hot.

Serve with sour cream or croutons (see Soup garnishes) and sprinkled with chopped parsley.

split pea soup

Serves: 8

Cooking time: 8–10 hours on Low

500g (1lb) split green peas

8 cups water or vegetable stock

1 ham bone

freshly ground pepper

1 onion, finely chopped

2 carrots, diced

2 celery stalks, sliced

1 bay leaf

salt and pepper to taste

croutons and freshly chopped parsley to serve

Soak peas overnight in plenty of water. Drain.

Place in slow cooker with water or stock and bone, pepper, onion, carrot, celery and bay leaf. Cover and cook on Low for 8 to 10 hours.

Remove bay leaf and bone. Remove meat from bone, cut into small pieces and return to soup. Add salt and pepper to taste.

Serve very hot, garnished with croutons and parsley.

french onion soup

Serves: 6-8

Cooking time: 6–8 hours on Low; 3 hours on High

6 cups beef stock

¼ cup butter

4 onions, thinly sliced

1½ teaspoons salt

1 tablespoon sugar

2 tablespoons plain flour

6–8 slices baguette

¾ cup grated cheese

½ cup dry white wine or 1 tablespoon brandy
   (optional)

Pour stock into slow cooker, cover and set on High.

Melt butter in another pan on medium heat. Add onions. Cover and allow to cook gently for about 15 minutes. Uncover and add salt, sugar and flour. Stir well, add to stock in slow cooker.

Cover and cook on Low for 6 to 8 hours, or High for 3 hours. Half an hour before serving add wine or brandy to soup.

Toast baguette slices under griller, sprinkle with cheese, return to heated griller until cheese is lightly toasted.

Serve in bowls, topping each with a slice of baguette with grilled cheese on top.

minestrone

If using dried beans, soak overnight and cook on High in water to cover for two hours, then drain. Ready cooked or canned beans may be added in the last hour of cooking.

250g (9oz) pancetta or thickly cut bacon

2 x 400g (14oz) cans cannelini beans

1 onion, finely chopped

1 clove garlic, crushed

2 celery stalks, diced

2 cups shredded cabbage

2 carrots, scraped and diced

400g (14oz) can peeled tomatoes

1 tablespoon tomato paste

½ cup spaghetti, broken in pieces

1 teaspoon dried oregano

2 teaspoons salt

freshly ground black pepper to taste

8 cups chicken or vegetable stock

chopped parsley, parmesan cheese and crusty bread to serve

Chop pancetta or bacon coarsely and place in slow cooker with beans, vegetables, spaghetti and seasoning. Add stock. Cover and cook on Low for 8 to 9 hours.

Serve topped with chopped parsely and parmesan cheese along with crusty bread.

spinach, lemon and lentil soup

Serves: 4-6

Cooking time: 8–9 hours on Low; 3–4 hours High

250g (9oz) green lentils

1 bunch English spinach

1 leek, finely chopped

2 cloves garlic, crushed

3 potatoes, peeled and chopped

2 carrots, sliced

1 bay leaf

2 sprigs thyme

4 cups vegetable stock

⅓ cup lemon juice, plus lemon wedges for
serving

1–2 tablespoons olive oil

Place lentils in a bowl, cover with cold water and leave to stand while preparing remaining ingredients. Wash the spinach thoroughly, trim and shred finely and set aside.

Drain lentils and place in slow cooker with leek, garlic, potatoes, carrot, bay leaf, thyme, stock and 2 cups water. Cook on Low for 8-10 hours or on High for 3-4 hours. Remove the lid and pull out bay leaf and thyme sprigs from soup. Add spinach and lemon juice and cook for 15 minutes, without covering, until spinach is wilted.

Check for seasoning, adding more salt and freshly ground pepper to taste. Ladle into bowls and drizzle each serving with a little extra virgin olive oil, serve with lemon wedges for squeezing over.

creamy mushroom soup

Serves: 4-6

Cooking time: 6–10 hours on Low; 2½–3 hours on High

375g (12oz) mushrooms, sliced

1 tablespoon butter

2 tablespoons plain flour

3 cups chicken stock

1 small onion, finely chopped

salt and freshly ground black pepper

½ cup cream (reduced fat or cooking cream)

1½ cups milk

fresh herbs, chopped, to serve

In a saucepan sauté sliced mushrooms in butter until softened, about 5 minutes. Stir in flour, place in slow cooker.

Add chicken stock, onion, salt and pepper; stir well. Cover and cook on Low for 6 to 10 hours, or on High for 2½ to 3 hours.

About 30 minutes before serving, turn to High. Add cream and milk to slow cooker.

Stir, cook until slightly thickened, and serve sprinkled with fresh chopped herbs such as parsley or chives.

smoked cod chowder

Serves: 4-6

Cooking time: 8–10 hours on Low; 3–4 hours on High

A hearty soup that is a meal in itself.

500g (1lb) smoked cod

2 large potatoes

1 leek, well washed and sliced

375ml (13 fl oz) fish stock

4 cups water

freshly ground black pepper

400g (14oz) can creamed sweet corn

½ cup cream

chopped parsley, to serve

Place fish in a large pan, cover with water and bring slowly to the boil. Simmer gently for 5 minutes. Remove from water. Remove any bones from fish, cut into bite-sized pieces and place in slow cooker.

Peel potatoes and cut into small dice, and add to slow cooker. Add leek, stock and water to slow cooker and stir well. Cover and cook for on Low for 8 to 10 hours, or on High for 3 to 4 hours.

Thirty minutes before serving, stir in sweet corn and cream. To serve, ladle into bowls and scatter with chopped parsley.

beetroot soup

1kg (2lb) beetroot, peeled and cubed

1 carrot, peeled and cut into chunks

1 parsnip, peeled and cut into chunks

1 potato, peeled and cut into chunks

1 leek, white part only, sliced

1 onion, peeled, chopped

⅓ cup (80ml) lemon juice

½ teaspoon allspice

1 small bay leaf

5 cups chicken or beef stock

salt and freshly ground black pepper

1 cup (250ml) light sour cream, to serve

⅓ cup chopped dill, to serve

crusty or rye bread, to serve

Place the beetroot, carrot, parsnip, potato, leek, onion, lemon juice, allspice and bay leaf in slow cooker with the stock. Cover and cook on Low for 10 to 12 hours, or on High for 4 to 5 hours.

Cool slightly, remove bay leaf, then blend in batches and season well with salt and freshly ground black pepper. Return to slow cooker and gently heat through.

Ladle into warmed bowls and garnish with sour cream and dill. Serve with rye bread.

beef &lamb

A slow cooker really shines when it comes to cooking meat. The long, slow cooking results in truly juicy, flavoursome meats and makes super-tender triumphs of the cheaper cuts.

For the working parent, a slow cooker makes having a good, nourishing meal ready, especially on school and work nights, so much easier. Stews, pot-roasts or casseroles can be assembled before you leave in the morning, placed in a slow cooker, and are ready to serve when you come home again.

Some vegetables can take as long to cook as meat, so cut them into small pieces and place covered with liquid on the bottom or around the sides of the pot. Browning meat is not necessary, however it does help to intensify flavour. Some slow cookers have a removable insert pan for searing that can be used on direct heat, which makes browning meat so much easier, and less washing up!

hearty beef casserole

Serves: 6

Cooking time: 7–10 hours on Low; 4–5 hours on High

1.5kg (3lb) beef (chuck, blade or shin)

⅓ cup plain flour

2 teaspoons salt

¼ teaspoon freshly ground black pepper

2 cups leeks or onions, sliced

3 or 4 celery sticks, sliced

3 potatoes, peeled and sliced

400g (14oz) can whole tomatoes

1 teaspoon oregano

2 cloves garlic, chopped

½ cup stock or water

2 tablespoons flour

3 tablespoons water

8 cherry tomatoes, quartered

chopped parsley to garnish

Wipe beef well, trim and cut into large cubes. Place meat in slow cooker. Combine flour with salt and pepper and toss meat with flour mixture to coat thoroughly.

Add remaining ingredients, except 2 tablespoons flour, water, and cherry tomatoes, in order listed; stir well. Cover and cook on Low setting for 7 to 10 hours, or High for 4 to 5 hours.

If gravy needs thickening, before serving, turn to High setting. Make a smooth paste of 2 tablespoons flour and the remaining water; stir into slow cooker, mixing well. Add cherry tomatoes. Cover and cook until thickened. Serve sprinkled with a generous handful of chopped parsley.

VARIATION:

Italian Beef Casserole: *Prepare as for Hearty beef casserole; substitute 4 carrots and 2 celery stalks, sliced, for potatoes. Substitute 2 cups tomato puree for stock. Add 1 teaspoon of oregano and 2 bay leaves.*

Greek Style Beef Casserole: *Make as per Hearty beef casserole. Instead of celery, substitute 1 eggplant, cut into large pieces. Cubed, boned lamb shoulder can be used instead of beef if liked.*

rich beef curry

This beef curry is rich and intense in flavour, which is achieved by frying the curry powder and other ingredients until lightly browned before adding the liquid and beef. The vinegar and tamarind adds a piquant flavour.

1kg (2lb) blade or chuck steak

2 tablespoons olive oil

10 curry leaves

¼ teaspoon fenugreek (optional)

1 large onion, finely chopped

4 cloves garlic, finely chopped

2.5cm (1 inch) piece of fresh ginger, grated

3 tablespoons curry powder

½ chilli, deseeded and sliced

2 teaspoons salt

1 tablespoon white vinegar

2 tablespoons tamarind puree

1 stick cinnamon

strip lemon rind

270ml (8fl oz) coconut milk

Cut the steak into bite-sized pieces. Heat the oil in a wide frying pan, add the curry leaves and fenugreek and fry for 1 minute. Add the onion, garlic, ginger and fry for a further 2 minutes. Add the curry powder and chilli and fry gently, stirring until lightly browned, about 3 to 5 minutes.

Add the salt and vinegar, then add the steak and cook over a high heat for 2 to 3 minutes, stirring to coat well with the curry mixture.

Transfer everything to a slow cooker and stir in the tamarind puree. Add the cinnamon stick and lemon rind. Cover and cook on Low setting for 6 to 10 hours or until meat is tender. Thirty minutes before serving, stir in coconut milk.

Serve with steamed rice, pappadams and a few sambals such as diced tomato with mint and chopped onion, cucumber and yoghurt, sliced banana with shredded coconut, and a selection of chutneys.

steak and kidney

This dish freezes beautifully.

1 ox kidney or 2 lamb kidneys

750g (1½lb) beef (shin or chuck), well trimmed
   and cut into cubes

1 onion, thinly sliced

3 tablespoons plain flour

1 teaspoon salt

½ teaspoon freshly ground pepper

1½ cups stock or water

Core the kidney using scissors and cut into small pieces.

Combine kidney, steak and onion in slow cooker. Add flour seasoned with salt and freshly ground pepper and toss to coat meat. Add stock. Cover and cook on Low setting for 6 to 10 hours, or High for 3 to 4 hours.

Serve with creamy mashed potato, boiled rice or squares of flaky or puff pastry that have been baked in a hot oven, or as a base for a steak and kidney pie.

beef strips in tomato cream

Serves: 20

Cooking time: 6–8 hours on Low; 3–4 hours on High

An ideal dish to serve as part of a party or buffet menu. Use a second slow cooker or rice cooker for cooking rice to accompany the beef. If making ahead and storing in the fridge, do not add sour cream until just before serving.

2-3kg (3-4lb) blade steak

½ cup plain flour

salt and freshly ground black pepper

3 teaspoons sweet paprika

60g (2oz) butter

2 tablespoons olive oil

2 onions, finely chopped

2 cloves garlic, crushed

2 x 400g (14oz) cans tomatoes

2 tablespoons Worcestershire sauce

500g (1lb) button mushrooms

2 cups diced green capsicum (bell pepper)

2 cups sour cream

chopped parsley, to serve

Cut beef into thin strips. Toss in flour seasoned with salt, pepper and paprika. Heat half the butter and oil in a frying pan and sauté meat in three or four lots until lightly browned, adding more oil and butter if necessary. Add to slow cooker.

Sauté chopped onion in a frying pan until golden and add to meat with garlic, canned tomatoes and Worcestershire sauce. Cover and cook on Low setting for 6 to 8 hours, or High for 3 to 4 hours or until meat is tender.

Slice mushrooms and sauté in remaining oil and butter, add to slow cooker. Taste for seasoning and set on Low. Add sour cream and stir just before serving.

Serve with rice garnished with liberal quantities of parsley.

beef strips and mushrooms

Serves: 6–8

Cooking time: 6–8 hours on Low; 3–4 hours on High

For a creamy sauce, ½ cup sour cream may be stirred into beef just before serving, and heated through.

1.5kg (3lb) chuck or blade steak

½ cup plain flour, plus 2 tablespoons extra

salt and freshly ground black pepper

½ cup chopped shallots (spring onions)

1 cup beef stock or water

1 teaspoon Worcestershire sauce

1 tablespoon tomato paste

250g (8oz) button mushrooms, sliced

½ cup red wine

chopped parsley and steamed rice, to serve

Cut steak into thin strips. Place in slow cooker.

Add ½ cup flour, salt and pepper and toss with beef to coat thoroughly. Add shallots.

Combine stock, Worcestershire sauce and tomato paste. Pour over beef and shallots; stir well.

Cover and cook on Low setting for 6 to 8 hours, or High 3 to 4 hours. Add mushrooms an hour before serving.

Thirty minutes before serving, turn to High setting. Make a smooth paste of red wine and extra 2 tablespoons flour; stir into slow cooker, mixing well. Cover and cook until thickened.

Serve with rice or noodles.

mediterranean beef with chick peas

Serves: 4–6

Cooking time: 8–10 hours on Low; 4–5 hours on High

Other canned legumes such as red kidney or cannellini beans may be used instead of chick peas.

1kg (2lb) lean stewing beef
   (chuck, blade or shin)

2 onions, sliced

2 cloves garlic, chopped

2 tablespoons olive oil

1 eggplant (aubergine), cubed

1 cup stock or water

3 tablespoons plain flour

1 teaspoon ground cinnamon

1 bay leaf

salt and freshly ground black pepper

400g (14oz) can chick peas

400g (14oz) can whole peeled tomatoes

mixed chopped herbs (parsley with a little
   oregano or thyme)

1¼ cups (250g) couscous to serve

Trim meat and cut into large cubes. In large frying pan brown meat, onions and garlic in oil; drain. Place in slow cooker. Add eggplant.

Combine stock, flour, cinnamon, bay leaf, salt and pepper and pour into slow cooker; stir well. Cover and cook on Low setting for 8 to 10 hours, or High for 4 to 5 hours.

Half an hour before serving turn to High, stir in chick peas and tomatoes and cook until heated through and flavours blended.

Meanwhile, place couscous in a heatproof bowl and pour over 1¼ cups boiling water. Cover and stand for 5 minutes. Fluff with fork. Season to taste.

Serve beef with a topping of chopped fresh herbs and couscous.

beef bourguignonne

Serves: 8

Cooking time: 8–10 hours on Low

Crusty baguette for mopping up the delicious gravy and a tossed green salad makes an ideal party meal.

3 bacon rashers or 100g (3½oz) pancetta, cubed

1.5kg (3½lb) beef (shin or chuck), cut into
  good sized pieces

⅓ cup plain flour

2 large carrots, peeled and sliced

1 medium onion, sliced

salt and freshly ground black pepper

1 cup beef stock

1½ cups red wine

2 tablespoons tomato paste

2 cloves garlic

pinch dried thyme

1 bay leaf

8 to 10 small pickling onions, peeled

2 tablespoons butter or 1 tablespoon oil

500g (1lb) mushrooms, sliced

freshly ground black pepper

Cook bacon in a large frying pan until crisp. Remove and drain. Dust beef with flour, and add to frying pan and brown well. Place browned beef with bacon in slow cooker.

Brown carrot and sliced onion. Season with salt and freshly ground pepper. Stir in flour. Add stock, mix well and add to slow cooker. Add wine, tomato paste, garlic, thyme and bay leaf. Cover and cook on Low setting for 8 to 10 hours.

In a frying pan sauté peeled onions in 2 tablespoons of butter or 1 tablespoon of oil, cook gently for 5 to 10 minutes, add mushrooms and toss in oil over heat for a few minutes. Add to slow cooker about 1 hour before serving.

To thicken gravy, turn slow cooker to High and cook without lid for 15 minutes.

Serve with steamed new potatoes, fluffy boiled rice or buttered noodles.

paprika beef casserole

Serves: 6

Cooking time: 6–10 hours on Low; 4–5 hours on High

Slow cooker recipe bases available from supermarkets make this dish quick and easy to prepare.

1.5kg (3lb) lean stewing beef (skirt, blade
  or shin)

2 tablespoons plain flour, seasoned

1 teaspoon sweet paprika

1 teaspoon smoked paprika

1 Slow Cooker recipe base, such as country beef,
  or ½ cup white wine and 1 cup stock

sliced mushrooms (optional)

1 onion, chopped

1 carrot, chopped

1 celery stalk, chopped

½ cup sour cream to serve (optional)

chopped chives to garnish (optional)

Trim beef and cut into large cubes, dust in flour combined with paprikas. Combine beef, recipe base, wine or stock and vegetables in slow cooker.

Cover and cook on Low for 6 to 10 hours, or on High for 4 to 5 hours. If using mushrooms, add about one hour before serving.

Serve with creamy mashed potato, a dollop of sour cream and sprinkling of chopped chives.

bachelor's hot pot

Serves: 4–6

Cooking time: 8–12 hours on Low; 3–5 hours on High

1kg (2lb) shin or chuck steak, or trimmed
    pork shoulder

3 tablespoons plain flour

salt and freshly ground black pepper

1 large onion, cut into eighths

3 carrots, peeled, and cut into strips

4 celery stalks, thickly sliced

2 teaspoons fresh thyme leaves

400g (14oz) can peeled tomatoes

1 cup beef stock or water

125g (4oz) sliced button mushrooms (optional)

Cut meat into cubes. Combine flour with salt and freshly ground pepper, toss with beef. Place coated beef pieces in slow cooker and add remaining ingredients, except mushrooms, stir well.

Cover and cook on Low setting for 8 to 12 hours, or High 3 to 5 hours. Add mushrooms an hour before serving.

beef shank
with vinegar gravy

Serves: 6

Cooking time: 8–12 hours on Low

1 onion	2 tablespoons malt vinegar
2 carrots	1½ cups water
2 celery stalks	salt
4 peppercorns	3 tablespoons tomato paste
2 whole cloves	1kg (2lb) beef shanks, cut in thick slices
2 tablespoons brown sugar	3 tablespoons plain flour

Peel and thinly slice onion and carrots; slice celery. Place in slow cooker with peppercorns, cloves, brown sugar, vinegar, water, salt and tomato paste, stirring well. Dust beef shanks in flour and place in slow cooker, being sure to cover with tomato paste mixture.

Cover and cook on Low for 8 to 12 hours. Fifteen minutes before serving, turn onto High and cook to thicken gravy, if required.

Remove meat with slotted spoon. Bone and cut the meat into small pieces, if you prefer, or serve the generous portions of beef on the bone.

Serve with creamy mash and your choice of vegetables.

lamb shanks with lemon

Serves: 4

Cooking time: 6–8 hours on Low

3 lamb shanks

3 tablespoons seasoned plain flour

1 tablespoon olive oil

1 onion, sliced thinly

400g (14oz) can tomatoes

1 clove garlic, crushed

1 teaspoon grated lemon rind

1 tablespoon lemon juice

½ bay leaf and stalk of parsley

2 carrots, sliced

salt and freshly ground black pepper

chopped parsley

Ask the butcher to cut each shank into 3 pieces. Dust the lamb in seasoned flour and brown lightly in oil. Browning can be omitted if time does not allow. Drain and place in slow cooker with onion, tomatoes, garlic, lemon rind and juice, bay leaf and parsley.

Scatter carrots around edge of slow cooker, ensuring they are covered with tomato liquid, cover and cook on Low for 6 to 8 hours. Thirty minutes before serving remove bay leaf, season to taste with salt and pepper. Turn onto High and cook, covered, for a further 15 to 20 minutes; uncovered if gravy needs to be thickened.

Top with a generous sprinkling of chopped parsley and serve with creamy mash.

lamb, olive and lemon tagine

Serves: 4

Cooking time: 8–10 hours on Low; 4½–5 hours on High

1 large lamb shoulder, boned and cubed

2 tablespoons olive oil

2 medium onions, quartered

2 cloves garlic, crushed

1 teaspoon ground cumin

2 teaspoons turmeric

juice of 1 lemon

½ cup chopped coriander (cilantro) or parsley

4 medium potatoes, quartered

½ cup green olives

1½ cups (300g) couscous

Remove any excess fat from lamb pieces. Heat oil in frying pan and brown lamb pieces, in batches, transferring as you brown to a slow cooker.

Add onion to frying pan with garlic, cumin and turmeric and cook another 30 seconds, stirring. Add 1 cup water and lemon juice and bring to the boil. Pour over lamb in cooker. Add coriander, reserving just a little for garnishing, a little salt and a good grinding of pepper. Stir, then cook for 2 hours on High. Add potatoes and cook for another 2 hours.

Add olives and cook without lid for another 30 minutes.

Meanwhile, place couscous in a heatproof bowl and pour over 1½ cups boiling water. Cover and stand for 5 minutes. Fluff with fork. Season to taste. Garnish tagine with remaining coriander and serve with couscous.

oxtail in white wine

Oxtail is very fatty, so take care to remove excess fat. If liked, this dish may be cooked a day ahead, chilled overnight and any excess fat lifted from the surface. Simply reheat on stove top or microwave.

2 oxtail, cut into pieces

seasoned plain flour

2 tablespoons olive oil

2 onions, chopped

2 cups white wine

1 bay leaf

a few stalks of parsley

1 clove garlic, crushed

1 tablespoon tomato paste

3 potatoes, thickly sliced

500g (1lb) fresh or canned tomatoes

Remove excess fat from oxtail. Dust in seasoned flour. Fry pieces in oil in a frying pan to brown. Transfer to a slow cooker. Drain off all but 2 tablespoons of fat.

Add chopped onion to frying pan and cook until golden. Add to oxtail in slow cooker. Add wine, bay leaf, parsley, garlic, tomato paste, potatoes and enough water to just cover ingredients.
Top with tomatoes and cook on Low for 10 to 12 hours or High for 5 to 6 hours until tender.

Skim off any excess fat. To thicken gravy, turn slow cooker to High and remove lid for 15 minutes. Check for seasoning. Serve with vegetables.

irish stew

Serves: 6

Cooking time: 8–10 hours on Low; 4–5 hours on High

Authentic Irish stew has twice the weight of potatoes and half the weight of onions to meat. You can use equal quantities of meat and potatoes to vary it, but in this case the gravy may need to be slightly thickened before serving.

1kg (2lb) lamb neck chops

2kg (4lb) potatoes

500g (1lb) onions

¼ cup plain flour

salt and freshly ground black pepper

1½ cups water

pinch of herbs

1 bay leaf

Trim excess fat from chops. Peel and slice the potatoes. Peel and slice onions. Place sliced onions and potatoes into a slow cooker. Dust meat in flour and add with remaining ingredients.

Cover and cook on Low for 8 to 10 hours, or High for 4 to 5 hours. This stew should not be thin, but should be thick, well seasoned and creamy. To thicken gravy, turn to High and cook, uncovered, for 15 minutes before serving.

highland hot pot

Serves: 4

Cooking time: 6–8 hours on Low; 3–4 hours on High

2 carrots

1 parsnip

1 small turnip

2 celery stalks

750g (1½lb) neck chops

¾ cup oatmeal

salt and freshly ground black pepper

1–2 tablespoons olive oil

2 cups beef or vegetable stock

extra oatmeal

30g (1oz) butter

Slice or dice vegetables and place into a slow cooker. Coat chops with oatmeal seasoned with salt and pepper. Heat oil in large frying pan and brown chops on both sides. Add scrapings of any of the toasted oatmeal from pan to slow cooker. Pour over stock. Cover and cook on Low for 6 to 8 hours, or High for 3 to 4 hours.

Put onto heatproof platter. Sprinkle top thickly with extra seasoned oatmeal. Dot with butter and place under griller until top is golden and crisp.

lamb pilaf

Serves: 4–6

Cooking time: 2–3 hours on High

1 small shoulder of lamb, boned

2 onions, chopped

80g (3oz) butter

1 cup long grain rice

2 cups stock

salt and freshly ground black pepper

1 tablespoon tomato paste

1 tablespoon melted butter

½ cup sultanas

chopped coriander (cilantro) and plain yoghurt
to serve

Cut the lamb into small cubes of about 1.5 cm (¾ inch). In a frying pan, sauté lamb and onions in half the butter until meat is brown and onions golden. Place together in slow cooker; add remaining butter to frying pan, fry rice and cook, stirring, until rice is coated with butter. Add to meat with stock, oregano and seasoning. Cover and cook on High for 2 to 3 hours. Give a light stir several times during cooking.

Combine tomato paste and melted butter and fork through pilaf with sultanas. Turn to High for 10 to 15 minutes. Sprinkle with chopped coriander and serve with plain yoghurt.

minced meats

———◆———

Meat loaf, meatballs and bolognaise are just a few of the many different minced meat dishes that may be made using a slow cooker.

Use topside or other lean meat for the best results.

Brown and drain fat from mince in a frying pan before adding to a slow cooker. Loaves, patties and minced meats cooked with breadcrumbs or rice do not require pre-browning – the bread and rice absorb fats and meat juices.

To maintain their firmness, meat loaves should be placed on a bed of sliced vegetables (potatoes, onions, carrots), which can absorb the juices and be served with the meat.

bolognaise sauce

Serves: 4–6

Cooking time: 10–12 hours on Low; 6–8 hours on High

A versatile sauce that can form the base of other dishes, including lasagne and cannelloni. You could also add kidney beans and chilli, and serve with guacamole, for a quick and easy chilli con carne (see recipe overleaf).

1kg (2lb) minced beef

large onion, finely chopped

2 cloves garlic, chopped

2 x 400g (14oz) cans diced tomatoes

2 tablespoons tomato paste

1 cup water

2 celery stalks, chopped

2 teaspoons salt

2 teaspoons fresh oregano, chopped

1 teaspoon fresh thyme, chopped

1 bay leaf

freshly ground black pepper

In a saucepan fry beef and onions, stirring well so that meat separates without forming lumps.

Put all ingredients in a slow cooker. Stir thoroughly. Cover and cook on Low for 10 to 12 hours, or High for 6 to 8 hours.

chilli con carne with guacamole

Serves: 4–6

Cooking time: 10–12 hours on Low; 6–8 hours on High

1 quantity Bolognaise sauce (see recipe)

1 cup cooked red kidney beans, drained and rinsed (see Bean salad)

1 large red chilli, de-seeded and sliced, or as to taste

1 large ripe avocado

¼ red onion, finely chopped

1 tablespoon lemon juice

sour cream to serve

Add kidney beans and chilli to one quantity Bolognaise sauce (see recipe).

For Guacamole, peel, stone and mash avocado, and mix through red onion and lemon juice.

Serve chilli con carne with guacamole and sour cream.

GUACAMOLE

peppered meat loaf

1kg (2lb) minced steak, or a mixture of pork and veal mince

250g (8oz) sausage mince, squeezed from good quality sausages

1 onion, chopped

3 cloves garlic, crushed

¼ cup tomato sauce

1 cup diced bread

2 eggs, lightly beaten

2 teaspoons Worcestershire sauce

salt and freshly ground black pepper to taste

2 potatoes, peeled and sliced

SAUCE

½ cup tomato sauce

2 tablespoons brown sugar

1½ teaspoons dry mustard

½ teaspoon nutmeg

Combine meats, chopped onion, crushed garlic, tomato sauce, bread, eggs and seasonings, mix well and shape into loaf.

Place sliced potatoes in bottom of slow cooker and place meat loaf on top.

Combine sauce ingredients and pour over meat loaf. Cover and cook on Low for 8 to 10 hours. Turn to High and remove lid for last hour.

Serve with potatoes.

stuffed capsicum (bell peppers)

Serves: 6

Cooking time: 6–8 hours on Low; 3 hours on High

6 capsicum (bell peppers; a mixture of red,
   green and yellow is attractive)

2 medium onions

2 cloves garlic

500g (1lb) minced beef

1½ teaspoons salt

½ teaspoon freshly ground black pepper

½ cup wine or stock

1 large ripe tomato, chopped

1 cup cooked rice

1 cup tomato juice or chicken stock

Slice tops off capsicum. Remove seeds and membranes.

Chop onions and garlic. Combine with mince, salt and pepper, wine and tomato. Add rice, toss well together then fill peppers with mixture.

Arrange stuffed capsicum in slow cooker. Pour over tomato juice or chicken stock. Cover and cook on Low for 6 to 8 hours, or on High for 3 hours.

Serve hot as a main dish, with a tossed green salad. Good, too, served cold.

swedish meatballs

Good quality minced meats, not too fatty, is what makes this dish such a treat. It's an excellent party dish – you can double the quantity, and it will keep just right on the Warm setting. The meatballs will have a finer texture if the meats are minced together twice.

1½ cups white breadcrumbs

1 cup cream or milk

500g (1lb) minced steak

250g (½ lb) minced pork or veal

1 egg, lightly beaten

1 medium onion, finely chopped

2 teaspoons salt

¾ teaspoon dill seed

¼ teaspoon allspice

pinch of nutmeg

45g (1½oz) butter

1 cup beef stock

freshly ground pepper

½ cup of cream, extra

Soak breadcrumbs in milk or cream for 5 minutes. Add meats, egg, onion, salt, herbs and spices. Mix well and refrigerate for 1 hour.

Shape mixture into balls about the size of a walnut and brown lightly in butter in a frying pan. Put meatballs into slow cooker as they are browned. (The browning step may be done in the oven: place in a pan and bake at 200°C/400° F for 15 minutes.)

Add beef stock and pepper to a slow cooker. Cover and cook on Low for 4 to 6 hours, or High for 1 to 2 hours.

Add extra cream before serving, turn to High for 10 to 15 minutes.

chicken

chicken cacciatore

1.5 kg (3lb) chicken pieces

salt and freshly ground black pepper

1 clove garlic, crushed

1 onion, chopped

½ cup wine or stock

3 tablespoons tomato paste

½ cup pitted green or stuffed olives

Rinse chicken pieces and dry with paper towel. Lightly season with salt and pepper. Place in slow cooker. Combine garlic, onion, wine or stock, tomato puree and olives, pour over chicken. Cover and cook on Low for 5 to 8 hours.

Serve with pasta of your choice, green salad and crusty bread if liked.

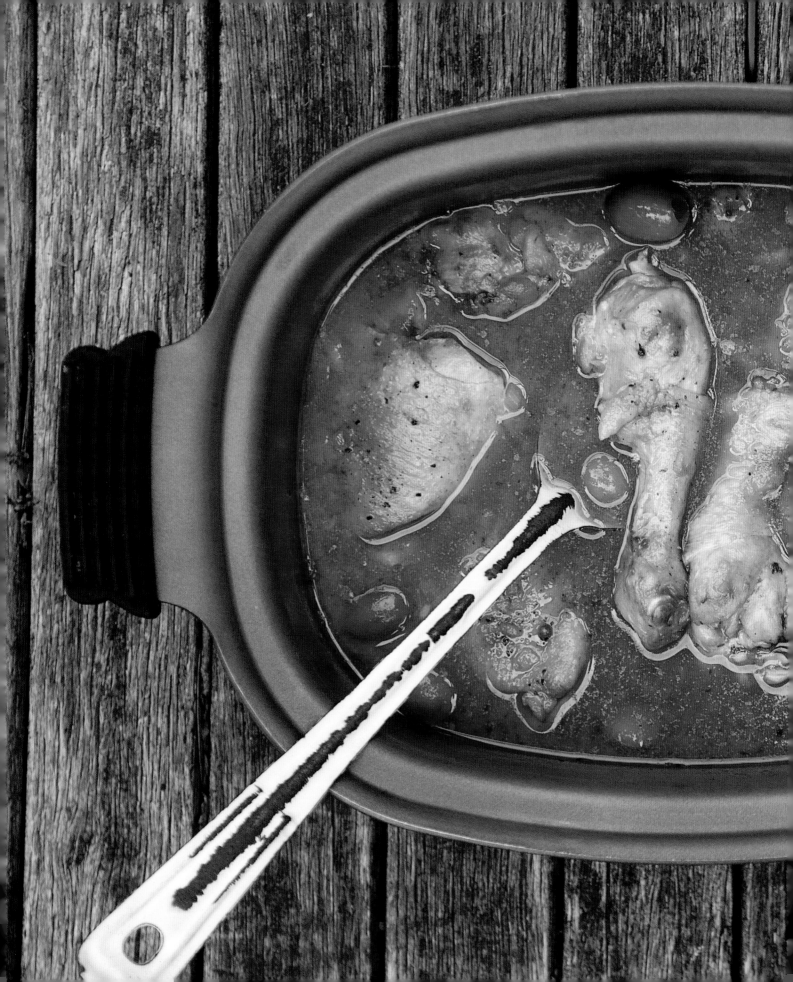

CHICKEN CACCIATORE

poached chicken

Serves: 4–6 each chicken

Cooking time: 7–8 hours on Low

Chicken poached in a slow cooker is delicious. It is a good idea to cook an extra one for use in salads and sandwiches. If you use the following basic poaching method, the cooking time will be the same even when the recipe is doubled. A 4-litre slow cooker will take two small chickens nicely. Place breasts outwards to each side.

1.5kg (3lb) chicken
salt and freshly ground black pepper
1 celery stalk
1 carrot

½ onion
1 bay leaf
1 cup chicken stock

Wipe chicken. Pat dry with paper towels and place in slow cooker. Season with salt and pepper, then place celery, carrot and onion around chicken, add bay leaf, and pour in stock. Cook on Low for 7 to 8 hours or until chicken is tender. Leave chicken in pot until cool enough to handle.

Lift chicken from slow cooker. Strain stock into refrigerator container and chill. Remove chicken meat from bones, keeping pieces as large as possible. Cover and chill. Use in salads, sandwiches, pies, in pasta, and other dishes where cooked chicken is required.

two-course chicken

This simple and delicious dish is two courses in one, with a soup made from the broth and then chicken, plenty of vegetables and pasta to follow.

1.5kg (3lb) chicken

2 carrots, quartered

2 onions, quartered

1 leek, sliced

2 celery stalks, sliced

bouquet garni (see Soups)

2 cups water

salt and freshly ground black pepper

½ cup pasta shapes, eg penne

parsley

Soup

1 cup water

juice of half a lemon

2 egg yolks

3 tablespoons cream

Wipe chicken and tie into a neat shape. Put the prepared vegetables in the bottom of a slow cooker. Add chicken, bouquet garni, water, salt and pepper.

Cover and cook on Low for 7 to 10 hours, or High for 3 to 4 hours. Add pasta for last hour of cooking with control turned to High. Pour off excess liquid from slow cooker and reserve; sprinkle chicken with chopped parsley to serve.

To make soup, strain broth into a saucepan; add water and heat with lemon juice. Beat yolks with cream, add a little of the hot broth and return to saucepan. Do not allow to boil. Check for seasoning with salt and pepper and serve hot.

coq au vin

3 rashers bacon, diced

4 eschallots (spring onion), sliced

1.5kg (3lb) chicken pieces

10 eschallots or small pickling onions, peeled

250g (8oz) whole button mushrooms

1 clove garlic, crushed

1 teaspoon salt

¼ teaspoon pepper

a few fresh thyme sprigs

8 small new potatoes, scrubbed and halved

1 cup red wine

1 cup chicken stock

In a large frying pan, sauté diced bacon and shallots until the bacon fat is clear. Remove and set aside. Pat chicken pieces dry, then add to the pan, brown well on all sides. Remove the chicken when it has browned, then set aside.

Put the peeled eschallots or onions, mushrooms and garlic in a slow cooker. Add the browned chicken pieces, bacon and shallots, salt and pepper, thyme, potatoes, wine and chicken stock. Cover and cook on Low for 7 to 8 hours, or High for 3 to 4 hours.

chicken in a bag

Serves: 4–6

Cooking time: 5–7 hours on Low

1.5kg (3lb) chicken pieces

⅓ cup plain flour

1 teaspoon salt

¼ teaspoon freshly ground black pepper

oven bag

2 medium onions, sliced

2 potatoes, sliced

1 tablespoon chopped fresh tarragon

250g (8oz) sliced mushrooms

½ cup water

thyme sprigs

Rinse chicken pieces and pat dry. Combine flour with salt and pepper. Place in oven roasting bag with chicken and toss around to coat chicken. Puncture 4 to 6 holes in bag and secure the opening with a tag.

Separate onion slices into rings and place in bottom of slow cooker. Add potatoes, mushrooms, tarragon and water, season with salt and pepper. Place chicken and thyme sprigs on top of vegetables in slow cooker. Cook on Low for 5 to 7 hours.

Serve chicken with vegetables and sauce.

chicken marengo

1.75kg (3½lb) chicken pieces

salt and freshly ground black pepper

plain flour

1 tablespoon oil

1 tablespoon butter

2 cloves garlic, finely chopped

bouquet garni (see Soups)

1 cup hot water

½ cup dry white wine

2 large tomatoes, peeled, chopped

12 mushrooms, sliced

Pat chicken dry, season with salt and pepper and dust with flour. In a heavy pan, heat the oil and butter. Add the chicken and cook over a medium heat until golden, turning frequently.

Transfer to slow cooker, add finely chopped garlic, bouquet garni, hot water, wine, peeled and chopped tomatoes and sliced mushrooms. Cover and set on Low for 6 to 8 hours, or High for 3 to 4 hours. To thicken sauce, turn to High and cook uncovered for 15 minutes. Extra sautéed mushrooms may be added just before serving

Serve with hot fluffy rice.

chicken with capsicum

Serves: 6

Cooking time: 5–8 hours on Low; 3–4 hours on High

6 chicken marylands, skin on

salt and freshly ground black pepper

¼ teaspoon ground cinnamon

⅓ cup plain flour

1 red capsicum (bell pepper), chopped

2 small onions, sliced

2 celery stalks, chopped

2 cloves garlic, chopped

250g (8oz) button mushrooms, sliced

¼ cup dry sherry

400g (14oz) can diced tomatoes

Pat chicken pieces dry, season with salt, pepper and cinnamon and dust with flour. Place capsicum, onions, celery and garlic in slow cooker. Add seasoned chicken pieces. Add mushrooms with sherry and tomatoes, stir well. Cover and cook on Low for 5 to 8 hours, or High for 3 to 4 hours.

Serve with hot noodles or fluffy rice and a crisp green salad.

pork & veal

pork chops and apples

Serves: 4–6

Cooking time: 6–8 hours on Low

4–6 pork loin chops, cut thick

2 cooking apples

30g (1oz) butter

¼ teaspoon ground nutmeg

salt and freshly ground black pepper

Trim pork chops and brown quickly in a frying pan to remove excess fat, drain well.

Peel, core and slice apples, arrange a layer of sliced apple in slow cooker, then add pork chops and repeat, finishing with a good layer of apple.

Dot with butter, sprinkle with nutmeg, salt and pepper. Cover and cook on Low setting for 6 to 8 hours.

Serve with creamy mash and red cabbage or coleslaw.

pork with spice, fruit and herbs

Serves: 6

Cooking time: 6–7 hours

900g (2lb) lean pork, cut into 2cm (1 inch) pieces

30g (1oz) flour

2 teaspoons curry powder

salt and freshly ground black pepper

2 tablespoons vegetable oil

2 onions, finely chopped

2 cloves garlic, crushed

75g (2½oz) each apricots, sultanas and fresh or dried dates

200g (7oz) sliced mushrooms

2 leeks, washed and thinly sliced

400g (14oz) can peeled tomatoes

1 cup chicken stock

2 teaspoons chopped oregano or majoram

coriander (cilantro) and couscous to serve

Dust the pork in flour seasoned with curry powder, salt and pepper until well coated. Heat the vegetable oil in a large frying pan, and fry the pork for 3 to 4 minutes, until browned all over. Transfer with a slotted spoon to a slow cooker.

Add the onion and garlic to the frying pan and fry over medium heat for 2 minutes until softened. Transfer to the slow cooker and add the fruit, mushrooms, leeks, tomatoes, stock, herbs and any remaining flour. Stir well to combine.

Cover and cook on Low for 6 to 7 hours. At the end of the cooking time, taste and adjust the seasoning if necessary. If liked, serve sprinkled with some chopped coriander and couscous.

pork chops with mushrooms

Serves: 4–6

Cooking time: 6–8 hours on Low; 3½ hours on High

4–6 pork chops

½ cup plain flour

1 tablespoon salt

1½ teaspoons dry mustard

2 tablespoons olive oil

1 clove garlic, crushed

500g (16oz) mushrooms

30g (1oz) butter

Dust pork chops in mixture of flour, salt and dry mustard. Brown in oil in a frying pan. Add garlic, fry gently until soft and lightly coloured. Place the browned pork chops and garlic in a slow cooker. Cover and cook on Low for 6 to 8 hours, or High for 3½ hours.

An hour before serving, stir in sliced mushrooms, which have been sauteed in butter. Serve with new potatoes and buttered beans.

veal and broad bean casserole

Serves: 4–6

Cooking time: 6–10 hours on Low

No need for side dishes with this one-pot wonder!

1kg (2lb) veal steak

¼ cup plain flour

1 onion, finely chopped

2 potatoes, quartered

2 carrots, finely sliced

1 small packet frozen broad beans, thawed

2 cloves garlic, chopped

1 green capsicum (bell pepper), deseeded and
    cut into strips

½ cup beef stock

2 teaspoons sweet paprika

1½ teaspoons salt

400g (14oz) can diced tomatoes

2 tablespoons chopped fresh parsley

Cut meat into large cubes, dust with flour and place in slow cooker with onion, potatoes, sliced carrots, beans, chopped garlic and capsicum.

Combine stock, paprika, salt and tomatoes and pour over meat and vegetables, stirring well. Cover and cook on Low for 6 to 10 hours.

To thicken gravy, 15 minutes before serving turn setting to High and cook uncovered until thickened. Sprinkle with parsley before serving.

osso bucco

Serves: 4

Cooking time: 8–9 hours on Low; 5 hours on High

4–6 slices veal shank, cut 3cm thick, with bone in

plain flour for dusting

salt and freshly ground black pepper

2 tablespoons olive oil

2 cloves garlic, chopped

1 onion, chopped

2 carrots, peeled and chopped

2 celery stalks, finely chopped

1½ cups dry white wine

1 bay leaf

1 sprig of rosemary leaves

5cm (2 inch) strip of lemon rind

400g (14oz) can diced tomatoes

mashed potato or soft polenta, for serving

GREMOLATA

½ cup finely chopped parsley

1 clove garlic, chopped

2 teaspoons grated lemon rind

Flour both sides of the veal shank slices, shaking off excess. Season with salt and freshly ground pepper to taste. Heat 1 tablespoon of the oil in a large frying pan on medium high heat and lightly brown the meat on both sides. Do not overcrowd the pan; you will have to do this in batches. Place the meat pieces in a slow cooker.

Add remaining oil to pan and sauté the garlic, onion, carrot and celery until wilted, about 5 minutes. Add to the veal in cooker with the wine, bay leaf, rosemary, lemon rind and tomatoes. Cover, and cook for 8-9 hours on Low; or on High for 5 hours.

Meanwhile, to make gremolata, mix together parlsey, garlic, lemon rind and place in a small bowl.

Serve osso bucco piping hot with mashed potato or soft polenta, letting everyone help themselves to the gremolata for sprinkling on top.

pork and veal terrine

Serves: 8

Cooking time: 7–8 hours on Low; 4–5 hours on High

Makes a delicious light lunch served with a tossed salad and crusty bread; or take to your next picnic and watch it disappear. If pork mince seems fatty, add 1 cup soft breadcrumbs to mixture. This is best made a day or two before eating.

750g (1½ lb) pork and veal mince

1 clove garlic

1 teaspoon salt

1 teaspoon chopped thyme

1 pinch ground cloves

freshly ground black pepper

1 egg, beaten

grated rind of half a lemon

¼ cup dry sherry or brandy

1 bay leaf

lemon slices to garnish

Grease a terrine dish or earthenware bowl that fits nicely into slow cooker. In a large bowl combine minced meat, garlic crushed with salt, herbs, a good grinding of pepper, beaten egg, lemon rind and sherry or brandy. Mix well with a wooden spoon. Spoon into prepared terrine. Smooth out and arrange bay leaf and lemon slices on top. Cover with a lid or a few thicknesses of aluminium foil.

Place ½ cup water in slow cooker, lower terrine into cooker, cover and cook on Low for 7 to 8 hours, or High for 4 to 5 hours. Remove terrine from cooker, cool with a weight on top, then chill. Serve in slices with crusty bread.

fish

———◦❂◦———

Fish is delicate and is best cooked for short periods and on a low temperature to preserve its moisture and fine texture.

Don't be afraid to lift off the cover and test the fish near the end of the specified cooking time. In timing, be sure to allow for the thickness of the fish. When cooking a whole fish slash it at the thickest part to allow it to cook evenly. When done the flesh should flake easily when tested with a fork, but it should still be moist. Remove fish from the slow cooker as soon as it is done.

CHINESE STEAMED FISH

FISH WITH BLACK BEAN SAUCE

chinese steamed fish

Serves: 4–6

Cooking time: 1½ hours on Low

2 whole fish (baby snapper), or 4 pieces of
    firm-fleshed white fish fillets

2 slices ginger

2 shallots (spring onion)

coriander (cilantro) sprigs

4 to 6 shallots (spring onion), green ends only

2 slices ginger, shredded

extra coriander

GARNISH

4 shallots, white ends only,
    shredded lengthwise

½ cup coriander sprigs

2 slices ginger, finely shredded

⅓ cup peanut oil

2 teaspoons soy sauce

Ask fishmonger to clean, scale and remove heads from fish if necessary to fit in slow cooker. Slash fish in thickest part and lightly salt inside and out. Place ginger strips, shallots and coriander sprigs in stomach cavity. Lay the green ends of the shallots, shredded ginger and more coriander in slow cooker to form a bed for fish. Place fish in slow cooker, side by side. Cover and cook on Low for 1½ hours. If cooking fish fillets, cook on Low for 1 hour.

Remove fish to heated serving plate and garnish with shredded white ends of shallots, coriander sprigs and shredded ginger. Mix oil and soy sauce and sprinkle over fish. Serve immediately with fluffy jasmine rice and steamed Asian vegetables, such as bok choy.

VARIATION: *Fish fillets with black bean sauce*

Authentic black bean sauce is available in the Asian section of most supermarkets, or from Chinese grocery stores.

Prepare fish fillets as for Chinese steamed fish, omitting coriander and ginger. After placing fish in slow cooker, pour black bean sauce over fish and garnish with white shallots. Cook on Low for 1 hour. Serve with rice and a salad of julienned Asian vegetables such as Chinese cabbage, carrot and snow peas with sesame oil and white vinegar dressing.

mediterranean fish stew

Serves: 4

Cooking time: 5 hours on Low

2 tablespoons olive oil

3 cloves garlic, crushed

1 small fennel bulb, thinly sliced

½ teaspoon dried chilli flakes

½ teaspoon sweet paprika

1 tablespoon caster sugar

120ml (4fl oz) dry white wine

250g (8oz) cherry tomatoes, halved

240ml (8fl oz) chicken or fish stock

1 tablespoon fresh basil, chopped

2 teaspoons fresh oregano

450g (1lb) firm-fleshed white fish fillets

225g (8oz) medium prawns, peeled
and deveined

small handful freshly chopped parsley, to serve

In a large frying pan, heat the olive oil over low heat. Add the garlic and the fennel. Sauté for 5 minutes until the fennel has softened.

Transfer to the slow cooker and add the chilli flakes, paprika, sugar, white wine, tomatoes, stock and herbs. Cook on low for 5 hours.

One hour before the end of the cooking time, taste and adjust the seasoning if necessary. Add the fish and prawns, and finish cooking. Just before serving, stir in the parsley.

hearty roasts & pot roasts

Cooking a whole joint or large piece of meat in a slow cooker proves just how succulent, juicy and melt-in-the-mouth meat can be. There is less shrinkage too. Then there's the richer, more flavoursome gravies because the seasonings and flavours of the meat have been kept in.

A pot roast in a slow cooker is an easy meal – as simple as seasoning the meat, putting it in a slow cooker and turning it on. If you want to cook vegetables at the same time, put sliced carrots, potatoes and onions on the bottom of the pot, meat on top, cover and cook on low.

Very little liquid is required, and for a crispy-browned finish, place meat in a hot oven or under a pre-heated grill for 15 minutes while you make the gravy.

pot-roasted leg of lamb

Serves: 4–6

Cooking time: 8–12 hours on Low (well-done); 5-6 hours on Low (pink meat)

1 leg of lamb

salt and freshly ground black pepper

4 onions

4 potatoes

2–3 cloves garlic

½ cup stock

If it is a large leg of lamb, ask your butcher to cut shank to make sure it fits into the slow cooker. Trim excess fat from lamb and season all over with salt and pepper.

Peel and thinly slice onions and potatoes and layer alternately on base of slow cooker, allowing room for the lamb. Place peeled and chopped garlic cloves on vegetables and place lamb on top. Pour stock over, cover and cook on Low setting for 8 to 12 hours, 5 to 6 hours for pink lamb.

If liked, just before serving place lamb under a hot grill or in oven to brown.

Serve lamb sliced with vegetables and juices from the slow cooker.

lamb with onion gravy

Serves: 4–6

Cooking time: 8–10 hours on Low (well done); 5–6 hours on Low (pink); 4 hours on High (medium)

1 leg of lamb, or lamb shoulder, boned and
    rolled
salt and freshly ground black pepper
2 cloves garlic, slivered

4 onions, sliced
½ cup water
1–2 tablespoons plain flour
2 potatoes, peeled and quartered (optional)

Trim excess fat from lamb. Lightly season with salt and pepper. Make slits with sharp knife into bone area, insert garlic slivers.

Place sliced onions into base of slow cooker. Place lamb on top of onions and add water. Arrange potatoes around the lamb, large potatoes may be cut int 6 or 8 pieces. Cover and cook on Low for 8 to 10 hours for well-done meat, 5 to 6 hours on Low for pink lamb, or 4 hours on High for medium.

Half an hour before required, remove lamb from slow cooker. Make a smooth paste with flour and a little water and stir until smooth, add to juices. Return lamb, cover, and turn to High for 30 minutes.

Place lamb in hot oven or under griller to crisp skin if liked.

stuffed shoulder of lamb

Serves: 6–8

Cooking time: 8–10 hours on Low

1.5-2kg (3-4 lb) lamb shoulder, boned

250g (8oz) sausage mince (use good-quality sausages)

1 onion, chopped

2 tablespoons fresh parsley

1 teaspoon fresh marjoram

1 teaspoon fresh oregano

1 clove garlic, chopped

1 onion, sliced

2 celery stalks, sliced

2 carrots, pared and sliced

Trim all excess fat from lamb shoulder.

To prepare stuffing, brown sausage mince and chopped onion in frying pan; drain well. Stir in herbs and garlic. Stuff lamb with the mixture, roll and fasten with skewers or string.

Place sliced onion, celery and carrots in slow cooker, then place stuffed and rolled lamb on top of vegetables. Season lamb with salt and pepper. Cover and cook on Low for 8 to 10 hours.

Serve lamb sliced, with the natural juices poured over vegetables and meat. If liked, arrange cut vegetables such as pumpkin, potatoes, onions and parsnips around meat and cook in slow cooker, or in the oven an hour before serving.

rosemary-stuffed lamb with white beans

Serves: 6

Cooking time: 7–10 hours on Low

1 lamb shoulder, boned

2 large onions

45g (1½oz) butter

1 cup fresh breadcrumbs

½ cup chopped parsley

2 teaspoons fresh rosemary leaves

salt and freshly ground black pepper

1 cup cooked white or cannelini beans

2 carrots, sliced

400 g (14oz) can whole tomatoes, cut
  into quarters

2 cloves garlic, crushed

1 cup stock or water

Trim lamb of excess fat and lay out on a board skin-side down. Chop onions finely and fry in butter until soft and transparent. Add half to breadcrumbs with parsley, rosemary and seasoning. Lay stuffing on lamb, roll into a neat shape and tie with string.

Place in slow cooker with beans, remaining onion, carrots, quartered tomatoes with juice from can, and garlic. Add stock. Cover and cook for 7 to 10 hours on Low.

Remove meat to a hot plate, lightly stir beans with juice from the meat. Cut lamb into thick slices and serve with a generous portion of beans.

lamb shoulder with anchovy stuffing

Serves: 6

Cooking time: 7–10 hours on Low

1.5kg (3lb) lamb shoulder, boned

salt and freshly ground black pepper

½ cup breadcrumbs

2 cloves garlic, crushed

2 anchovy fillets, finely chopped

2 onions, sliced

½ cup stock

Trim excess fat from lamb. Lightly season with salt and pepper. Combine breadcrumbs, garlic and anchovy, spread over inside of shoulder. Roll up into neat shape, tie with string.

Place sliced onions in base of slow cooker. Place lamb on top of onions. Add stock. Cover and cook on Low for 7 to 10 hours.

Serve lamb sliced with onions, potatoes and steamed green vegetables. If liked, the gravy may be thickened with a little flour added to the juices, and the slow cooker turned to High for 15 minutes or until thickened.

pot-roasted chicken

Serves: 4–6

Cooking time: 7–8 hours on Low; 3–4 hours on High

For a crispy finish, cut chicken into joints and place under a pre-heated griller for 5 minutes while you make the gravy. If one chicken is not enough for your family buy 2 smaller birds and fit them into the slow cooker back to back; the breasts will touch the sides of the slow cooker.

1.8kg (3½lb) or larger chicken

salt and freshly ground black pepper

2 tablespoons chopped fresh oregano or
  tarragon

2 cloves garlic, chopped

6 small onions, peeled

12 baby carrots, scrubbed

12 baby potatoes, scrubbed

Wash chicken and pat dry. Season chicken with salt and pepper. Sprinkle half the oregano and garlic inside cavity.

Place chicken in the slow cooker, sprinkle with remaining oregano and garlic. Arrange vegetables around the sides of the chicken. Cover and cook on Low for 7 to 8 hours, or on High for 3 to 4 hours. Transfer chicken to carving board. Skim fat and pour pan juices into sauce bowl, or use to make gravy. Carve bird. Serve with vegetables and juices or gravy spooned over chicken.

Crispy chicken: *For a crispy finish, cut chicken into joints and place under a pre-heated griller for five minutes, or while you make gravy.*

CRISPY CHICKEN

chicken with gravy

Serves: 4-6

Cooking time: 7-8 hours on Low; 3-4 hours on High

Cook chicken as per Pot-roasted chicken. The juices in the baseof the slow cooker may be thickened with a little flour blended with water first then added to the slow cooker; turn the pot to High until the gravy thickens (about 10 minutes).

For creamy gravy, add half a cup of cream to chicken juices when thickening.

For mushroom gravy, add sliced mushrooms sautéed in butter to the chicken juices when thickening the gravy.

lemon roast chicken

Serves: 4–6

Cooking time: 7–8 hours on Low; 3–4 hours on High

Prepare chicken according to Pot–roasted chicken recipe. When chicken is placed in the slow cooker cover breast with 5 thick slices of lemon, and squeeze juice from the rest of the lemon over chicken.

Cover and cook on Low for 7 to 8 hours, or High 3 to 4 hours. The lemon slices from the chicken breast may be chopped and added to the gravy, which can be made in any of the ways suggested for Pot–roasted chicken.

stuffed roast chicken

Serves: 4–6

Cooking time: 8–10 hours on Low

1.8kg (3½lb) chicken

60g (2oz) butter

1 medium onion, chopped

3 celery stalks with leaves, chopped

125g (4oz) sliced mushrooms

2 cups soft breadcrumbs

2 tablespoons chopped parsley

1 tablespoon chopped sage

freshly ground black pepper to taste

½ cup chicken stock

1 teaspoon butter

paprika

Rinse chicken well and pat dry; remove any excess fat.

In frying pan melt butter, sauté onion, celery and mushrooms. Toss in breadcrumbs, parsley, sage, pepper and stock. Stir until stuffing is moistened.

Loosely stuff chicken. Tie legs loosely. Place chicken in slow cooker and rub breast with 1 teaspoon butter; sprinkle with paprika.

Cover and cook on Low for 8 to 10 hours, then remove chicken to a heatproof platter. For a crisp brown skin place in a hot oven for 10 to15 minutes.

Garnish with parsley sprigs and serve with vegetables of your choice. For roast vegetables, prepare and place in oven an hour before serving.

thai pork roast with garlic

Serves: 8

Cooking time: 7–10 hours on Low; 3–4 hours on High

Delicious roast pork loin or neck, fragrant with cumin and garlic. Cut a lovely fresh pineapple into spears to accompany the pork, or add to the sauce before serving to heat through

2kg (4lb) pork loin, neck or rolled, boned
    shoulder

2 teaspoons ground cumin

6 cloves garlic, crushed with a little salt

plenty of freshly ground pepper

1 pineapple

⅓ cup soy sauce

¼ cup white vinegar

⅓ cup brown sugar

½ cup chopped fresh coriander (cilantro)

Remove the rind from the pork. It can be baked separately in a hot oven if you want crackling. Combine the cumin, garlic and pepper and rub well into meat. Cut the skin from the pineapple and use some of it to cover the piece of pork. Place the pork in a slow cooker and cook for 6 to 7 hours on Low; 3 to 4 hours on High, until almost tender. Discard the pineapple skin then baste the meat with a mixture of the soy sauce, vinegar and sugar. Return to the cooker for a further 2 to 3 hours, basting frequently. Remove pork to a platter, skim fat from sauce in slow cooker and serve as gravy with the meat. Meanwhile, cut the skinned pineapple into spears or rings and leave fresh, or saute in butter and use to garnish the pork along with the sprigs of coriander. Serve the pork carved into slices with steamed rice.

glazed corned beef

Serves: 8–10

Cooking time: 8–12 hours on Low; 4–5 hours on High

2-2.5kg (4-5lb) corned beef (rolled or silverside, with a thin layer of fat on top)

1 bay leaf

1 medium onion, sliced

2–3 strips fresh orange peel

3 whole cloves

1½ cups water

GLAZE

3 tablespoons orange juice

3 tablespoons honey

1 tablespoon Dijon mustard

Place all ingredients (except corned beef and glaze) in slow cooker, mix well. Add corned beef with fat side up. Cover and cook on Low for 8 to 12 hours or on High for 4 to 5 hours, or until fork tender.

Remove meat from liquid. Place corned beef on heatproof platter. Score fat of corned beef in diamond shapes. Insert additional cloves to decorate. Prepare glaze by mixing all ingredients together until smooth and blended, spoon over corned beef.

Bake in a moderately hot oven (200°C/400° F) for 20 to 30 minutes, basting occasionally with glaze. Serve hot with creamy mashed potatoes, steamed carrots and cauliflower gratin. Also a delicious cold meat for sandwiches.

beef pot roast

Serves: 6

Cooking time: 8–10 hours on Low (well-done); 6–7 hours on Low (medium); 5–6 hours on High

2–3 potatoes

2–3 carrots

2 onions

salt and freshly ground black pepper

2kg (4lb) topside or rolled rib of beef

½ cup water or beef stock, or white or red wine

extra salt and pepper to taste

mustard, to serve

Trim all excess fat from meat. Cut vegetables into thick slices and place in base of slow cooker.

Season beef with salt and pepper, then place in slow cooker. Add water or stock, and extra salt and pepper to taste.

Cover and cook on Low for 8 to 10 hours for well-done meat, 6 to 7 hours for medium, or on High 5 to 6 hours. Remove meat and vegetables with large spoon. Serve the meat carved into thin slices along with vegetables and mustard.

italian pot roast

Serves: 6–8

Cooking time: 8–10 hours on Low

2kg (4lb) topside or rolled rib of beef

2 onions

2 cloves garlic

1 large celery stalk

2 teaspoons fresh oregano

2 rashers pancetta or bacon

½ cup plain flour

1 punnet cherry tomatoes

fresh basil leaves, shredded, to serve

Trim all excess fat from meat.

Finely chop one onion, the garlic, celery, oregano and bacon, mix well. Lightly flour meat; rub with chopped vegetable mixture. Slice remaining onion; place in the slow cooker. Place meat on onion. Cover and cook on Low for 8 to 10 hours. An hour before serving, add cherry tomatoes.

Serve beef sliced with the juices from slow cooker, which may be thickened with a little flour just before serving. Serve with pasta or crusty bread and a green salad.

POT ROAST VARIATIONS:

German: Add 3–4 medium dill pickles and 2 tablespoons fresh dill.

French: Add 1 cup fresh sliced mushrooms, 500g (1lb) small peeled onions and 1 cup red wine.

lamb pot roast

Serves: 6–8

Cooking time: 8–10 hours on Low

2kg (4lb) shoulder of lamb

2–3 potatoes

2–3 carrots

1–2 onions

salt and freshly ground black pepper

½ cup water or beef stock

extra salt and pepper to taste

Ask your butcher to bone and roll lamb. Cut vegetables into thick slices and place in bottom of the slow cooker .

Season lamb with salt and pepper, then place in slow cooker. Add water or stock and extra salt and pepper to taste.

Cover and cook on Low for 8 to 10 hours for well-done meat, 6 to 7 hours for medium, or on High 5 to 6 hours. Remove meat and vegetables with large spoon. Serve carved into slices.

pork pot roast

Serves: 6–8

Cooking time: 8–10 hours on Low

A joint of pork cut from the leg or the shoulder, boned and rolled or tied in a neat shape may be cooked as for Beef pot roast.

2–3 potatoes

2–3 carrots

1–2 onions

salt and freshly ground black pepper

2kg (4lb) pork leg or shoulder

½ cup water or beef stock

leaves from 1 rosemary sprig

extra salt and pepper to taste

Ask your butcher to bone and roll pork shoulder. Trim all excess fat from meat. Remove rind and if liked, score and rub with salt, then cook in a very hot oven for 30 minutes before servinc to make crackling. Cut vegetables into thick slices and place in bottom of the slow cooker .

Season pork with salt and pepper, then place in the slow cooker. Add liquid, rosemary and extra salt and pepper to taste.

Cover and cook on Low for 8 to 10 hours. Remove meat and vegetables with large spoon. Serve with steamed vegetables of your choice.

beef and beer pot roast

Serves: 6–8

Cooking time: 8–10 hours on Low

1.5-2kg (3-4 lb) topside, rolled rib of beef or
    silverside

salt and freshly ground black pepper

2 onions, sliced

1 cup beer

1 tablespoon brown sugar

1 clove garlic, crushed

1 tablespoon fresh thyme

4 peppercorns

1 bay leaf

3–4 potatoes, peeled and quartered

3–4 carrots, scraped and halved

2 tablespoons plain flour

salt and freshly ground black pepper to taste

Trim excess fat from meat, season with salt and pepper. Place onions in slow cooker with meat.

In a bowl combine beer, brown sugar, garlic, thyme, peppercorns and bay leaf. Pour over meat. Tuck vegetables around meat, cover and cook on Low for 8 to 10 hours. Remove meat and vegetables and keep warm.

Skim excess fat from liquid in slow cooker and measure 1½ cups liquid into a small saucepan. Blend ¼ cup cold water with flour, stir into pan juices and bring to the boil. Season if necessary.

Slice meat and serve with gravy and vegetables. If liked, swap potatoes for new potatoes, steamed or microwaved, and lightly buttered.

vegetables & side dishes

A big dish of steaming, hot, flavoursome potatoes for a crowd; scalloped potatoes; potatoes layered with onions, bacon and cheese; and ratatouille … these vegetable dishes are great in a slow cooker. You can put a whole butternut squash in a slow cooker, and cook it all day on Low—when you lift the lid it will be done. Cut it in two, scoop out the seeds, cut in wedges and top with butter, pepper and salt and serve to a hungry family.

Carrots, parsnips and turnips do well in a slow cooker, alone or combined. Simply slice, barely cover with water or stock, season with salt, pepper and a sprinkle of herbs, cook on Low for 8 to 10 hours, drain, mash with butter, pepper and salt.

Ideal to serve with barbecued meats.

baked potatoes

Perfect for the barbecue. Just take a slow cooker filled with cooked potatoes right to the table and lift the lid!

Fill the slow cooker with scrubbed and buttered medium-sized new potatoes. It will hold about 12. Sprinkle with salt. Cover and cook on low for 8 to 10 hours, or until potatoes are tender. For family meals, just cook the required number of potatoes, you get the same excellent result. Serve with butter, or sour cream and chopped chives.

scalloped potatoes

Serves: 6

Cooking time: 6–10 hours on Low; 3–4 hours on High

3 rashers bacon, diced

2 medium onions, thinly sliced

4 medium potatoes, peeled and thinly sliced

2 cups grated cheese

salt and freshly ground black pepper

30g (1oz) butter

Butter the slow cooker dish or a heatproof dish that fits into the slow cooker. Using half the ingredients, put a layer of potatoes, bacon, onions and cheese in dish. Season to taste with salt and pepper and dot with butter. Repeat layers, finishing with cheese. Be sure the potatoes are completely covered. Season and dot with butter. Cover and cook on Low for 6 to 10 hours, or High for 3 to 4 hours.

boulangère potatoes

Serves: 6

Cooking time: 8–10 hours on Low

1kg (2lb) potatoes

500 g (1lb) onions

1-2 cups stock, to cover

salt and freshly ground black pepper

Grease the slow cooker dish or a heatproof dish that fits in a slow cooker with a little butter. Peel potatoes and onions and slice thinly. Layer them alternately, seasoning each layer, and finishing with a layer of potatoes. Pour stock over vegetables, to cover. Cover and cook on Low for 8 to 10 hours.

If liked, place under a hot grill or in a pre-heated very hot oven (230°C/450°F) to brown top afterwards.

Season to taste and serve with meat or chicken of your choice.

ratatouille

Serves: 4–6

Cooking time: 7–8 hours on Low; 3–4 hours on High

2 medium-sized eggplant (aubergines)

6 small zucchini (courgettes)

2 capsicums (bell peppers)

6 tomatoes

2 onions

2 cloves garlic

salt and freshly ground black pepper

½ cup olive oil

Cut eggplant into cubes, slice zucchini, capsicum and tomatoes. Slice onion finely, crush garlic. Place onion in slow cooker first, then add remaining ingredients. Cover and cook on Low overnight for 7 to 8 hours, or on High for 3 to 4 hours. Vegetables should be soft but not mushy. Mix lightly and add more salt and pepper if necessary. Serve with rice, couscous or pasta, with grated parmesan or use as a filling for omelettes.

baked sweet potatoes

Cooking time: 4–6 hours on Low; 1 hour on High

Place washed, unpeeled, small sweet potatoes in slow cooker. Add about ¼ cup of water. Cover and cook on High for 1 hour, then turn to Low for 4 to 6 hours or until the potatoes are tender.

Split lengthwise, and serve hot with butter.

swiss cheese fondue

Serves: 6

Cooking time: 1 to 1½ hours on Low

Fondues are a great way to entertain or add some fun to a cold winter evening. Guests spear bread on the end of a fork, swirl it around in the melted cheese and then savour the delicious combination. It's another way of using the versatile slow cooker, for the small amount of heat required to keep the cheese mixture at the right consistency can be maintained on the Low or Warm setting.

1 clove garlic, cut

1 cup dry white wine

500g (1lb) Swiss cheese (half gruyère and half emmental), shredded

3 teaspoons cornflour

2 tablespoons kirsch (optional)

a good pinch granted nutmeg (optional)

freshly ground black pepper

crusty baguette, cubed

Rub inside of slow cooker bowl with a cut clove of garlic. Pour in wine, turn to Low; toss cheese in cornflour, add to wine in slow cooker. Heat mixture for 1 to 1½ hours when cheese will be softened and beginning to melt. Stir with a wooden spoon until cheese is melted and creamy. Stir in kirsch and season with grated nutmeg, if liked, and freshly ground black pepper.

Spear pieces of baguette on long forks and dip into the fondue as desired. Turn slow cooker to Warm; as the fondue is getting to the end turn slow cooker off; it will still keep the mixture warm.

Points to watch if a cheese fondue is to be kept smooth and uncurdled:
Cheese must be melted over Low heat.

The fondue must be stirred gently but constantly to get a creamy mixture once the cheese has melted. When ready to eat, keep fondue on the lowest possible heat setting of the slow cooker.

bean salad

Serves: 6

Cooking time: 2–3 hours on High, and 6–8 hours on Low

500g dried beans (cannellini, red kidney,
    or pinto beans)

½-1 cup finely chopped onions or eschallots
    (spring onions)

½ cup finely chopped parsley

DRESSING

⅓ cup malt vinegar

⅔ cup olive oil

1 teaspoon salt

1 clove garlic, finely chopped

1 teaspoon Dijon mustard

good grinding of black pepper

Soak beans overnight, rinse and place in slow cooker, adding water to cover. Cook for 2-3 hours on High, then on Low for 6-8 hours. Allow to cool. Mix dressing ingredients together very thoroughly. Toss drained cooked beans in dressing, and sprinkle with finely chopped onions or shallots and parsley. Pre-cooked or canned beans can be substituted for dried beans for a quick and delicious salad, without cooking.

chilli beans and bacon

Serves: 6

Cooking time: 2–3 hours on High, and 6–8 hours on Low

500g (1lb) cooked kidney beans

4 cups cold water, or enough to cover beans

1 large onion, coarsely chopped

400g (14oz) can diced tomatoes

2 garlic cloves, crushed

1 medium red chilli, seeded and chopped

125g (4oz) pancetta or bacon, diced

2 teaspoons salt

Soak beans overnight in enough water to cover. Drain and rinse, then place into slow cooker. Add water, cover and cook on High for 2 to 3 hours.

Pour off water. Add remaining ingredients and cover and cook on Low for 6 to 8 hours. For vegetarians, omit pancetta. Delicious as a topping for baked potatoes. Adjust chilli as desired.

dhal

500g (1lb) dried red lentils

7 cups chicken or vegetable stock

30g (1oz) butter

1 tablespoon curry powder

5 curry leaves (optional)

1 onion, chopped

1 clove garlic, crushed

1 carrot, diced

1 large celery stalk, sliced

salt and freshly ground black pepper to taste

250g (½lb) cherry tomatoes

¼ cup chopped coriander (cilantro), to serve
  (optional)

Wash lentils, place in slow cooker with stock.

Melt butter in saucepan, add curry powder, curry leaves if using, onion, garlic, carrot and celery. Cook gently for 5 to 10 minutes. Add to lentils.

Cover and cook on Low for 8 to 10 hours, or on High for 3 to 4 hours. Add cherry tomatoes in the last hour.

Season to taste, ladle into warmed serving bowls and scatter with chopped coriander. Serve with steamed basmati rice, or as an accompaniment to curry.

pumpkin and spinach risotto

Serves: 4

Cooking time: 3–4 hours on High

2 tablespoons olive oil

4 shallots (spring onions), finely chopped

2 cloves garlic, finely chopped

240g (8½oz) arborio (risotto) rice

400–450g peeled and chopped butternut
  (or other pumpkin)

240ml (8fl oz) dry white wine

1 litre (34fl oz) chicken stock

salt and freshly ground black pepper to taste

250g (8½oz) fresh baby spinach leaves, washed

2 tablespoons freshly chopped sage

½ cup grated parmesan, plus extra grated
  parmesan cheese, to serve

Heat oil in a small saucepan, add the shallots and cook over medium heat for 4 minutes until softened. Add the chopped garlic, cook for another minute. Transfer to the slow cooker, add the rice and butternut pumpkin and turn them around in the shallots and oil until well coated. Add the wine and stock, and season with black pepper and salt. Cover and cook on high for 3 to 4 hours.

Fifteen minutes before the end of the cooking time, add the spinach leaves, chopped sage and ½ a cup of parmesan and mix them in. Add salt and pepper to taste. Serve sprinkled with the extra grated parmesan.

desserts

There is hardly a person who doesn't look forward to dessert: baked apples, traditional creamy rice custards, bread and butter puddings—family favourites everyone enjoys. A slow cooker makes them so easily. It also cooks delicious fresh fruit dishes like Pears in wine and sweet, spiced, dried fruits. Once you get into the swing of using your slow cooker for everyone's favourite course, you'll be able to adapt your own time-tested recipes to the slow cooker.

baked apples

Serves: 6–8

Cooking time: 8 hours on Low

6–8 medium baking apples

3 tablespoons mixed dried fruits

¼ cup brown sugar

1 teaspoon cinnamon

2 tablespoons butter

Wash and core apples. Mix dried fruits and half the sugar; fill centres of each apple with the mixture. Sprinkle with cinnamon and remaining sugar and dot with butter. Place in slow cooker and add ¼ cup water. Cover and cook on Low overnight for 8 hours, and serve hot with ice-cream, cream or custard. Also delicious with breakfast cereal, topped with yoghurt.

stewed apples

6 large cooking apples, peeled, cored
   and sliced

1 cup water

1 teaspoon ground cinnamon

½–1 cup caster (super fine) sugar

Put all the ingredients into the slow cooker. Cover and cook on Low overnight or for 8 to 10 hours. Serve hot or cold, with cream or topping of your choice.

apples and rice

4 cooking apples

½ cup rice

1 cup water

1 cup milk

2 tablespoons caster (super fine) sugar

½ teaspoon ground cinnamon

30g (1oz) butter

Peel and core the apples, leaving them either whole or in halves. Place them in the slow cooker. Wash the rice and add to the slow cooker with the apples, water and milk. Sprinkle with sugar and cinnamon and put a knob of butter on each apple. Cover and cook on High 3 to 4 hours.

Serve with cream, or topping of your choice.

gingered pears

Ripe pears will cook in less time, 4 to 6 hours on Low. If it is not convenient to make a syrup, place sugar, ginger and water in slow cooker first, cover and turn to High while preparing the pears. If you are cooking on Low, remember to adjust the setting when the pears go in.

¾ cup caster (super fine) sugar

2 teaspoons ground ginger

2 cups water

6 pears

2 teaspoons arrowroot or cornflour

1 tablespoon sliced preserved or fresh ginger

Place sugar, ground ginger and water in saucepan, boil to make a syrup. Meanwhile peel pears, leaving stems intact. Place in slow cooker, pour over syrup, cover and cook on Low for 6 to 8 hours, or on High for 3 to 4 hours. Remove to serving dish.

Soften arrowroot with a little water, stir into liquid in slow cooker, turn heat to High, and cook until thickened. Add sliced ginger and spoon over pears. Serve with vanilla ice cream, or topping of your choice.

creamed rice pudding

Serves: 6

Cooking time: 4–6 hours on Low; 1–2 hours on High

2½ cups cooked rice

1 cup evaporated milk

⅓ cup cream

1 cup milk

⅓ cup brown sugar

2 tablespoons butter

½ teaspoon vanilla

1 teaspoon nutmeg

⅓ cup raisins

Thoroughly combine rice with other ingredients. Pour into lightly greased slow cooker. Cover and cook on Low for 4 to 6 hours, or on High for 1 to 2 hours. Stir during the first thirty minutes. Add more milk if mixture becomes too thick. Serve hot.

pears in red wine

Serves: 6–8

Cooking time: 4–6 hours on Low

2 cups dry red wine

1 cup caster (super fine) sugar

1 stick of cinnamon or 4 whole cloves

6–8 medium pears

4 thin strips lemon peel

Put wine, sugar and spice into the slow cooker. Cover and set on High. Meanwhile, peel pears, keeping whole and leaving stems on. Put into slow cooker, turning to coat well with liquid. Add lemon peel. Cover, turn down to Low and cook for 4 to 6 hours (6 to 8 hours for firmer fruit), turning pears occasionally to coat with wine mixture.

Serve with wine syrup poured over pears. Syrup may be thickened with 2 teaspoons arrowroot blended with water; in this case add arrowroot to slow cooker after removing pears, turn to High and cook until sauce thickens.

rice custard

2 tablespoons rice

2½ cups water

pinch salt

3 eggs

3 tablespoons caster (super fine) sugar

3 cups milk

½ teaspoon vanilla extract

30g (1oz) butter

grated nutmeg

½ cup raisins

Wash rice, cook in boiling salted water for 12-14 minutes, until tender. Drain well and put into greased bowl or heatproof dish that will sit in slow cooker. Beat eggs with sugar, add remaining ingredients. Stir into rice. Cover bowl with foil or a small plate. Pour 1 cup hot water into slow cooker, place bowl of rice custard into slow cooker. Cover and cook on Low for 6 to 8 hours.

Serve warm.

bread and butter pudding

Serves: 6

Cooking time: 3–4 hours on High

12 thin slices of baguette, buttered

½ cup mixed dried fruit (currants, sultanas and chopped peel)

3 tablespoons caster (super fine) sugar

3 eggs

2½ cups milk

1 teaspoon vanilla bean paste

Halve bread slices and arrange in layers, buttered side up, in special slow cooker cake pan or in greased ovenproof dish that will fit easily into the slow cooker. Sprinkle each layer with fruit and sugar. Lightly beat eggs, milk and vanilla until mixed, strain over bread in dish. Allow to stand for 10 minutes to 1 hour. Cover bowl with foil or lid. Put 1 cup hot water in slow cooker, place bowl of pudding into slow cooker, cover and cook on High for 3 to 4 hours.

simple plum pudding

Serves: 6

Cooking time: 2¼–3 hours on High

60g (2oz) butter

3 tablespoons brown sugar

1 cup mixed dried fruits

½ cup chopped dates

2 teaspoons grated lemon rind

1 teaspoon bicarbonate of soda

1 cup boiling water

1 cup self-raising flour

1 teaspoon mixed spice

¼ teaspoon salt

Grease pudding basin or slow-cooker cake pan. Put butter, sugar, mixed fruit, dates, lemon rind and bicarbonate of soda into a large mixing bowl and pour in boiling water. Stir well and allow to cool slightly. Sift in flour, spice and salt and stir lightly until blended. Pour into prepared basin or cake pan.

Place 1 cup of boiling water in slow cooker and turn to High. Cover basin with double layer of greaseproof paper and tie with string, or put lid on slow-cooker cake pan. Place pudding in slow cooker, cover and cook for 2 ½ to 3 hours on High.

Remove pudding from slow cooker and allow to stand for 5 minutes before turning out and serving with custard or cream.

baked custard

3 eggs

2 tablespoons caster (super fine) sugar

2 cups milk

½ teaspoon vanilla extract

sprinkling of nutmeg

Beat eggs with sugar, add milk and vanilla, mix until incorporated into egg mixture. Place in a greased heatproof bowl or dish, selecting one that will fit into slow cooker. Sprinkle with nutmeg. Cover custard with foil or small plate. Pour 1 cup hot water into the slow cooker, place bowl of custard into slow cooker. Cover and cook on Low for 6 to 8 hours.

Serve warm or cold.

warm spiced fruit

Serves: 6–8

Cooking time: 7–8 hours on Low; 3–4 hours on High

An easy fruit dessert, also ideal as a topping for cereal

1 cup dried prunes

1 cup dried apricots

1 can pineapple chunks, undrained (optional)

2 cups water

Put all ingredients in slow cooker. Cover and cook on Low overnight for 7 to 8 hours, or on High for 3 to 4 hours. Serve warm with sour cream and a sprinkle of cinnamon or nutmeg. Other dried fruits of your choice, such as apples, peaches and cranberries, can also be used.

winter fruit
with almonds

Serves: 6–8

Cooking time: 6–8 hours on Low; 4–6 hours on High

A wonderful combination of plump dried fruits, apples and nuts.

2 Granny Smith apples

250g (8oz) dried prunes

250g (8oz) dried figs

250g (8oz) dried apricots

½ cup caster (super fine) sugar

½ cup raisins

2 tablespoons blanched, slivered almonds

Peel, core and slice apples. Place with remaining ingredients, except almonds, in slow cooker. Add water to just cover fruit and cook on Low for 6 to 8 hours, or on High for 4 to 6 hours. Cool, spoon into serving dish and scatter the almonds over the top. Serve warm, or chilled with thick fresh cream, or yoghurt.

orange spiced prunes

Serves: 6

Cooking time: 8 hours on Low

500g (1lb) pitted dessert prunes

grated rind of 1 orange

1 tablespoon caster (super fine) sugar

1 cinnamon stick

1 cup water

Place prunes with remaining ingredients in slow cooker. If necessary add a little more water just to cover prunes. Cover and cook on Low for 8 hours.

This is delicious served warm or cold, or as a topping for breakfast cereals.

chocolate self-saucing pudding

Serves: 4

Cooking time: 5–6 hours on Low; 3½ hours on High

An all-time favourite dessert that can be made in advance.

100g unsalted butter, melted

½ cup milk

1 egg

1 cup self-raising flour

2 tablespoons cocoa powder

½ cup caster (super fine) sugar

TOPPING:

2 tablespoons cocoa powder

1 cup firmly packed brown sugar

2 cups boiling water

In a mixing bowl, combine butter, milk and egg.

In a separate large bowl, sift flour and cocoa together and mix in the sugar.

Gradually add the wet ingredients to the flour mixture and mix well. Spoon into a greased 6 cup pudding basin, and place in the slow cooker.

To make topping, combine the cocoa and brown sugar together, sprinkle over the top of pudding. Carefully pour boiling water over the mixture.

Cover and cook on Low for 5 to 6 hours, or on High for 3½ hours.

Serve hot with ice cream or cream.

dundee cake

250g (8oz) butter

¾ cup caster (super fine) sugar

grated rind and juice of 1 orange

5 eggs

2¼ cups plain flour

1 teaspoon baking powder

½ teaspoon salt

½ cup blanched almonds

¾ cup sultanas

¾ cup currants

¼ cup chopped mixed peel

¼ cup glace cherries

extra almonds

Grease a special slow cooker cake pan or a round 18cm (7 inch) cake tin and line with 2 thicknesses of baking paper. Grease the paper again.

Cream butter and sugar with the grated rind of the oranges, reserving juice to use later. Beat in eggs one at a time. Sift flour, baking powder and salt. Chop almonds. Mix into flour with the fruit. Stir into creamed mixture with the orange juice.

Turn into the prepared tin. Smooth the top and decorate with the extra almonds. Place in a slow cooker. Place a slow cooker cake pan lid on, or if using an ordinary cake tin cover top with 4 to 6 paper towels. Cover with a clean, folded tea towel and cook on High for 4 to 5 hours. Do not be tempted to open the lid until the last hour to check the cake, as lifting the lid may lengthen the cooking time by 20 minutes. If cake doesn't look brown enough, leave in turned-off slow cooker with the lid on. It will continue to cook gently. Remove when it looks done.

jams & chutney

three-fruit marmalade

Cooking time: 8–10 hours

The fruit should be transferred to a large heavy saucepan after being cooked in slow cooker as it will not get to the full rolling boil essential for good marmalade and jam making.

2 lemons

1 sweet orange

1 grapefruit

3½ cups water

6 cups caster (super fine) sugar

Wash and dry fruit. Slice lemons and orange finely. Reserve pips and put into a muslin bag. Peel the rind from grapefruit with vegetable peeler; shred and add to other fruit. Peel pith from grapefruit, chop pith finely and add to pips in muslin. Slice flesh finely and add to other fruit. Tie up muslin. Place fruit and muslin bag into slow cooker, pour over water, cover with lid and cook on Low setting for 8 to 10 hours or overnight.

Next day, remove muslin bag. Measure pulp; warm sugar on a tray in the oven, and for each cup of pulp add 1 cup sugar. Place pulp and sugar in a large saucepan and stir until sugar has dissolved, then bring to the boil and cook rapidly until setting point is reached—about 15 to 20 minutes. Take pan off heat and cool for about 15 minutes to distribute peel evenly through marmalade. Ladle marmalade into warmed dry, sterilized jars. Cover and seal.

cumquat conserve

1 kg (2lb) cumquats

1 lemon

3½ cups water

6 cups caster (super fine) sugar

Make as for Three-fruit marmalade. Wash, halve and pip cumquats, slice the lemon; tie lemon and cumquat pips in muslin bag. Place fruit in slow cooker, add water, cover and place on Low setting for 8 to 10 hours. Then proceed following the steps for the Three-fruit marmalade.

curried fruit chutney

Cooking time: 1½ hours on Low plus 1½ hours on High

Fruit chutney is an ideal accompaniment to cold meats, curries and cheese. It will keep stored in airtight containers, and once opened, in the refrigerator. Fruit chutney makes a good condiment for ham, pork chops or pork roast, fish and many other foods—use your creativity and imagination.

500g (1lb) coarsely chopped dried apricots

2 cups boiling water

3 apples, coarsely grated

1 cup of coarsely chopped pitted prunes or dates

½ cup of raisins

1 medium onion, peeled and chopped

¾ cup of brown sugar

2½ cups of apple cider vinegar

½ teaspoon of ground ginger

¼ teaspoon of cayenne pepper

1 teaspoon of salt

Soak apricots in boiling water for 30 minutes.

Pre-heat slow cooker on High. Mix together the soaked apricots with remaining ingredients. Place them in the slow cooker and cook covered on High for 1½ hours, then on Low for another 1½ hours. During the last hour, check fruit to ensure it is not overcooking (the fruits should be tender but not lose their shape).

Once the chutney is finished cooking, spoon chutney into sterilized jars while still hot and cover with lids. They should form a vacuum seal during cooling. Once opened, store in the fridge.

spanish quince paste

Cooking time: 10–12 hours on Low

Quince paste can be served with coffee as a sweet meat or cheese, going particularly well with soft, creamy cheese. When served as a sweetmeat the paste may be dusted with caster (super fine) sugar.

Here is an easy way to make this excellent Spanish sweetmeat—the long, slow cooking of the quinces in a slow cooker develops a rich ruby or mahogany colour.

4–6 quinces

½ cup water

white sugar

Rub the quinces with a cloth to remove the furry down. Put them whole and unpeeled into slow cooker with ½ cup water (it will take 4 to 6, depending on the size of the quinces). Cover, turn heat to Low and cook overnight or for 10 to 12 hours. The quinces will become a deep ruby colour and should be soft without breaking up.

When quinces are cool enough to handle, slice them, without peeling, into a bowl, discarding the cores and any bruised or hard pieces. Put the sliced fruit through a food mill or sieve. Weigh the puree and add an equal weight of white sugar. Boil in a heavy pan, stirring nearly all the time until the paste begins to candy and come away from the bottom as well as the sides of the pan. Use a long-handled wooden spoon for stirring. The boiling paste bubbles and spits so take care.

Turn off the heat and continue stirring until the boiling has ceased. Fill shallow rectangular earthenware or tin dishes with the paste. Leave to get quite cold. Next day put these moulds into the lowest possible oven setting until the paste has dried out and is quite firm (about 2 to 3 hours). On bright sunny days the paste may be left in the sun to dry out—this is the traditional way it is done in Spain.

Turn out the slabs of paste, wrap them in baking paper or foil, and store them in an airtight container.

index

Published in 2012 by
New Holland Publishers (Australia) Pty Ltd
Sydney • Auckland • London • Cape Town

First published in 1976 as The Margaret Fulton Crock-Pot Cookbook
by Paul Hamlyn Pty Ltd.

1/66 Gibbes Street Chatswood NSW 2067 Australia
218 Lake Road Northcote Auckland New Zealand
86 Edgware Road London W2 2EA United Kingdom
80 McKenzie Street Cape Town 8001 South Africa

A record of this book is held at the National Library of Australia

ISBN: 9781742571553

Publisher: Fiona Schultz
Publishing Manager: Lliane Clarke
Editor: Bronwyn Phillips
Designer: Celeste Vlok
Photography: Karen Watson
Food Stylist: Katherine McKinnon
Food Assistant: Jodi De Vantier
Chef: Andrew Ballard
Recipe Consultant: Suzanne Gibbs
Production Manager: Olga Dementiev
Printer: Toppan Leefung Printing Ltd (China)
10 9 8 7 6 5 4 3 2 1

Our thanks to Suzanne and Robert Gibbs, and Louise Fulton Keats.
Also to Nicole Norton from Sunbeam.
All recipes photographed were cooked in Sunbeam slow cookers, 5.5L Manual Slow Cooker, Sunbeam 5.5L Electronic Slow Cooker and the Sunbeam SecretChef 5.5L Electronic All-in-one Sear and Slow Cooker. Visit www.sunbeam.com.au for more information and recipes.